The RAF Pathfinders

Bomber Command's Elite Squadrons

Martyn Chorlton

Foreword by
The Revd Canon Michael Wadsworth

COUNTRYSIDE BOOKS
NEWBURY BERKSHIRE

First published 2012
© Martyn Chorlton 2012
Reprinted 2014

COUNTRYSIDE BOOKS
3 Catherine Road
Newbury, Berkshire

To view our complete range of books,
please visit us at
www.countrysidebooks.co.uk

ISBN 978 1 84674 201 9

*Cover picture showing Lancasters of 83 Squadron
crossing the enemy coastline
is from an original painting
by Colin Doggett*

Produced through MRM Associates Ltd., Reading
Typeset by CJWT Solutions, St Helens
Printed by Berforts Information Press, Oxford

Contents

Contents (cont.)

Foreword

The River Ouse bisects pathfinder country. To the north of the river, acres of the ancient forestlands darken the road with shadow but suddenly through a gap in the trees the far horizon is glimpsed across the dead-flat peaty land that slopes down towards the south-west. Rain draining off the airfields could make the sleepy, almost motionless, Ouse into a torrent that overflooded its banks and filled the shady lanes with deep mud even in high summer. For there were many airfields, or, put another way, just one airfield, and over it the winged monsters slid, as once went the pterodactyls that are still found fossilized in the nearby chalk quarries.

From Len Deighton's book, *Bomber*

The **Pathfinder Force of the RAF** was an attempt to bring order and meaning and effectiveness into a situation where only a third of a bomber force on raids in the recent past had bombed within five miles of the target. These shortcomings were the subject of the Butt Report published in the second half of 1941. Although the C. in C. of Bomber Command, Arthur Harris, did not agree with a special force of élite aircrew to find targets and mark them, he was overruled by Portal and Churchill, and the maiden operation of PFF took place against Flensburg on the German-Danish border on 18 August 1942, seventy years ago.

Four squadrons formed the new PFF, and aircraft from these four squadrons went to war. There were Lancasters from 83 Squadron at Wyton, Stirlings from 7 Squadron at Oakington, Wellingtons from 156 Squadron at Warboys, and Halifaxes from 35 Squadron at Graveley.

Everyone of these 'Pathfinder squadrons' (for that is what they became), was supplied by a different bomber group and, in January 1943, Pathfinders officially became 8 Group, with A/V/M Donald Bennett, the most efficient airman in the service, as Group Commander.

What follows now is an adapted excerpt from a sermon I preached on Sunday, 16 August, 1992, in a service to commemorate the 50th Anniversary of the formation of the Pathfinder Force. As we are now celebrating the 70th Anniversary of the foundation and formation of the Pathfinder Force (1942–2012), we need to take a good long look at the bravery, motivation, and story of these men. Sadly, of course, the great majority of those original aircrew present in the congregation of 1922, are no longer with us.

Let us now praise famous men
And our fathers in their generations. (Ecclesiasticus 44:1)

'Let us now praise famous men.' We are here to praise your discipline, your courage and devotion, your high morale, and your decisive contribution to the peace we now enjoy, fragile though it is, fragile as peace always is. We are here to remember your Group Commander, A/V/M Bennett, who saw to it, after that first Pathfinder-led raid on Flensburg, seventy years ago, that this fledgling force was given the equipment, the instruments to do the job, and saw to it too that only the best, the very best, came to Pathfinders from the main force squadrons; saw to it that courage and efficiency were the prime requirements for membership of the force, and not just the gratuitous accident of being known by the families of the great and the good.

What no one could ever know then, what is so hard to take in today, is that from Warboys airfield, where my father was, which has now, like Graveley, Bourn, Gransden Lodge, Downham Market, Little Staughton and others, gone under the plough (in appropriate prophetic tradition) – from that airfield, of 93 seven-men Lancaster crews, posted to the squadron between June, 1943, and the time the squadron moved to Upwood in March/April 1944, only 17 survived. The rest took off into the dark, and fell from the night skies over Germany; a few aircrew, a very few aircrew from these missing aircraft, became prisoners of war. The majority perished. It was the same at other Pathfinder stations. After his experience at Oakington, where he was stationed with 7 Squadron, H. E. Bates captures the tears of things in an elegiac story called "There's no future in It", in which an anxious father tries to dissuade his only daughter, the apple of his eye, from marrying a Pathfinder aircrew member. Oakington lost three C.O.s in succession during the dark days of late 1943 and early 1944, while 97 Squadron at Bourn, on an appalling night in December 1943, lost one Lancaster over Berlin, and seven crashing in the fenland fog on their return (accounting for the lives of 49 men, while six were injured). That same night, "Black Thursday" it was called, Warboys lost another Lancaster, which crashed on the Ely to Sutton road, while Gransden Lodge lost one aircraft which came down in fog barely half a mile from this cathedral church. "It's a great life, if you don't weaken," muttered one Australian navigator in the Sergeants' Mess at Warboys after one such "shaky do". The rest of what that Australian navigator said I cannot repeat in this cathedral church. "Let us now praise famous men, And our fathers in their generations."

Twenty-five minutes it took to run the gauntlet of the Berlin defences from end to end at full stretch. And as you took off into all this, there was that little knot of WAAFs and well-wishers waving you off. For we must not forget the WAAFs and their contribution. It was hard for the WAAF who had to drive a crew out to their aircraft to realise – and she did realise it – that for many of them she was the last female, and the last person, they would see on earth.

Among that host of well-wishers waving off the aircraft would be not a few girlfriends and wives; even though wives were not allowed to live within five miles of an operational station, some were smuggled in to the host villages close by your aerodromes nonetheless. At Warboys, beyond the church and cemetery, a wire barrier blocked the ordinary road, as the runway ran across it. At that barrier many a girl stood waving her handkerchief, as her chevalier in bulky flying clothes waved to her from the astrodome on taking off.

A widow wrote that she saw her young husband off at King's Cross Station on the 5 am to Huntingdon, and by 11 pm of the same day he was running into the flak barrage that blew him and his crew up over Berlin. And you ground crews, who literally kept the Pathfinder offensive on its feet, know all about those many unspoken "goodbyes", as you saw your aircraft with your crew turn round on the hard standing to join other Lancasters on the perimeter track, as they taxied out to take off for the night's operations. And how you waited, you ground crew, over there near the flight huts for the overdue aircraft to come in, only turning away when it became obvious that the aircraft had not enough fuel to keep in the air.

In our remembering, and in the church's remembering, I cannot help but see that figure, that young man, who set his face and his feet towards Jerusalem, and who knew what awaited him there. He knew what he had to do, and he knew he had to do it, as the words of the Creed run, "for us men and for our salvation". In the background of my glimpse of this figure picking up his own cross and going on, I see too, on an occasion like today's, all those crews at the height of the bomber battle for Berlin, taking off in those appalling weather conditions in the winter of 1943/1944 to shatter the enemy and shorten the war, no matter what it cost in terms of their own lives.

You must go back to your homes in many parts of the world with tremendous pride that you are remembered, that your name lives for evermore, and that anyone who sets his face towards his own individual Jerusalem can look back at you in those days, pursuing your task in the cold upper skies, or, maybe, circling low as the crew of a Master Bomber, or racing for Berlin in a Mosquito as part of the Light Night Striking Force, and doing each and all of these tasks to shorten the conflict in Europe, and, if spared, to return to your homes. A farmer on his tractor in New Zealand, an accountant in Vancouver, a teacher from Queensland, a bank official from Johannesburg, a government official from the Bahamas all of them now retired, can remember what they did with you, when they were young.

I close with a poem, for it expresses perfectly what many of the families of these *men felt, in their bereavement, all that time ago. It is by John Pudney, and it describes you, preparing to go on a raid all those years ago.*

> *'Empty your pockets, Tom, Dick and Harry,*
> *Strip your identity, leave it behind.*
> *Lawyer, garage hand, grocer, don't tarry*
> *With your own country, with your own kind.*
>
> *Leave all your letters. Suburb and township,*
> *Green fen and grocery, slip-way and bay,*
> *Hot spring and prairie, smoke-stack and coal tip,*
> *Leave in our keeping while you're away.*
>
> *Tom, Dick and Harry, plain names and numbers,*
> *Pilot, observer, and gunner depart.*
> *Their personal litter only encumbers*
> *Somebody's head, somebody's heart.'*

God bless you all. You are part of my life, and I wish you happy landings.

The Revd. Canon Michael Wadsworth

Introduction

Leading the way

The introduction of a Pathfinder Force from August 1942 undoubtedly helped to change the fortunes of Bomber Command. While not overnight, the command was steadily transformed from a token 'hit and miss' force to one that could deliver anything from a single bomb to hundreds of tons of bombs accurately onto a target anywhere in Western Europe.

The concept of an elite group was reluctantly accepted by Sir Arthur Harris, the C-in-C (Commander-in-Chief) of Bomber Command. 'Cherry-picking' crews was frowned upon at the time but it would have to be the crème of crews that had the skills needed. Chief scientist and adviser Sir Henry Tizard summed up the predicament that Harris feared by saying, 'I do not think the formation of a first XV at rugby union makes little boys play any less enthusiastically!' The men of 8 Group were described by their C-in-C, AVM (Air Vice Marshal) D. Bennett as '... serious, studious, meticulous – and gallant. Their contribution to victory was unique'.

The Butt and Cherwell reports

The effectiveness of Bomber Command against the enemy during the early war years was very difficult to gauge. Only analysis of post-attack aerial photography captured by PRU (Photographic Reconnaissance Unit) aircraft could evaluate whether or not a raid was successful. From the start of the war through to the end of 1940, Bomber Command bravely tackled dangerous targets with the Blenheim, Hampden, Whitley and Wellington. These were good aircraft in their own right but did not have the ability to deliver a significant bomb load. However, when the heavier bombers such as the Manchester, Stirling and Halifax entered service in 1941, the amount of bombs dropped on the enemy increased dramatically. Approximately 13,500 tons of bombs were dropped by Bomber Command during the whole of 1940. This same figure was reached by June 1941 and was surpassed by another 18,000 tons before the year was out. Despite this encouraging increase, photographs of the target areas showed no significant increase in damage caused from the previous year.

Questions were now being asked at very senior levels about the very reason for Bomber Command's existence, let alone its effectiveness. The production of bombers, airfields and the panoply of equipment and personnel that went with it used a colossal amount of the country's war material; it needed to be justified and fast.

A report into Bomber Command was initiated by German-born Lord Cherwell (Frederick Alexander Lindemann, 1886–1957) who, at the time, was chief scientific adviser to the Cabinet and a close personnel friend of Winston Churchill (1874–1965). Cherwell's private secretary, David Benusson-Butt (1914–1994) was given the task of compiling the report based on an assessment of 633 target photographs from 100 bombing raids. He then studied aircrews' claims of those same targets and his results sent shudders through Bomber Command and Parliament.

The report was published on 18 August 1941 and it revealed a catalogue of failure for Bomber Command. The report began with the fact that, of those aircraft which actually claimed to have bombed the target, only a third had bombed within five miles. The truth of the matter was that only one in six bombed within a 75-square-mile zone around the target and only 66% of aircraft dispatched claimed to have actually bombed the target. The target types were broken down as follows: French ports were successfully bombed by two out of three aircraft, Germany was one out of four and the Ruhr specifically was down to only one in ten aircraft bombing the target. When operating under a full moon, two out of five targets were claimed hit and in a new moon period the figure slumped to one in fifteen.

Despite venomous disagreement by senior RAF personnel, in hindsight, it appears that the Butt report was actually quite complimentary. The simple conclusion of the report stated that of those aircraft which claimed to have reached the target, only one third really did. Post-war analysis of RAF bombing raids between May 1940 and May 1941 not only confirmed the Butt report findings but showed that 49% of bombs actually fell in open country. Butt's exclusion of aircraft which suffered mechanical or equipment failure, enemy action, poor weather conditions or getting lost, veiled the fact that the real figure was approximately 5% of bombers dropping their bombs within five miles of the target.

Bomber Command quickly dismissed Butt's statistics as incorrect and, in response, commissioned their own report. The report was drawn up by the Directorate of Bombing Operations on 22 September 1941 and it applied considerable more theory than that adopted by the Butt report. Basing its findings on damage inflicted on British cities and towns, the report claimed that, with a force of 4,000 aircraft, the 43 towns in Germany populated by 100,000 people or more could be destroyed in a very short period. This finding was boldly backed up by ACM (Air Chief Marshal) Sir Charles Portal (1893–1971) who stated that a force of this size could win the war within six months!

These optimistic figures were doubted by many from Churchill downwards but Portal forcefully claimed that Bomber Command's role in the war effort was crucial in aiding the British and any future Allied forces back into Europe and eventual victory. While many still disagreed with bombing policy at the time, a compromise was reached and Bomber Command's allocation of war material continued.

Debate continued within the House of Commons and one particular speech by the MP for the University of Cambridge, Professor A. V. Hill (1886–1977) went as follows: *'The total (British) casualties in air-raids since the beginning of the war are only two thirds of those we lost as prisoners of war at Singapore. The loss of production in the worst month of the Blitz was about equal to that due to the Easter holidays. The Air Ministry have been too optimistic. We know most of the bombs we drop hit nothing of importance.'*

On 30 March 1942, in response to continued concerns from the Butt report, Lord Cherwell published his own report known as the De-housing Paper. Once again, after studying the effect of bombing on the British population, the main conclusion of the paper was that the demolition of people's houses actually had a greater effect on their morale than even the death of a relative. Cherwell estimated that, on average, for every one ton of bombs dropped on a built-up area, approximately 20 to 40 houses were destroyed, rendering between 100 and 200 people homeless. With regard to the RAF bomber at the time, each aircraft completed an average of fourteen operational sorties. He went on to estimate that the new aircraft entering service could carry an average of three tons each. This would equate to an average of 40 tons dropped by each aircraft during its operational lifetime. This, in turn, should result in a single aircraft, if dropping its bombs on a built-up area, causing between 4,000 and 8,000 people to become homeless. Cherwell went on to predict the amount of bombers produced up to the middle of 1943 as at least 10,000 aircraft. To quote from the paper, *'If even half the total load of 10,000 bombers were dropped on the built-up areas of 58 principal German towns, the great majority of their inhabitants (approx. one third of the German population) would be turned out of house and home.'*

The paper effectively supported a strategic 'area bombing' offensive and gave both Portal and the Secretary of State, Sir Archibald Sinclair, another great supporter of Bomber Command, the justification they needed to keep the Command alive. The strategic bombing technique would also compensate for the Command's current difficulties in bombing targets accurately, the theory being that if they missed the industrial target, there was every chance that a house would be destroyed instead.

Bomber Command was by no means out of the woods yet and, like the Butt report before it, the De-housing Paper now took its turn to be criticised. Its most vocal critic was Professor Patrick Blackett (1897–1974), the chief scientist to the Royal Navy. Blackett claimed that the paper's estimate of what could be achieved by Bomber Command was at least 600% too high! Blackett also supported the scientific advisor, Sir Henry Tizard's (1885–1959) stance to scale back Bomber Command's efforts in favour of supplying more resources to the Royal Navy and Army. Tizard claimed that the only benefit of strategic bombing was its ability to drain the enemy's resources in defending Germany. This, he stated, could still be achieved by a considerably smaller bomber force attacking the same targets.

The debate rumbled to the point where a High Court judge, by the name of Mr Justice Singleton, was brought in by the Cabinet to preside over the different viewpoints. Singleton then delivered his report on 20 May 1942, which went as follows:

> '*I do not think it (the bombing offensive) ought to be regarded as of itself sufficient to win the war or to produce decisive results; the area is too vast for the effort we can put forth: on the other hand, if Germany does not achieve great success on land before the winter, it may well turn out to have a decisive effect, and in the meantime, if carried out on the lines suggested, it must impede Germany and help Russia. If Germany succeeds in her attack on Russia there will be little apparent gain from our bombing policy in six months' time, but the drain on Germany will be present all the time: and if Russia stands it will remain a powerful weapon on our hands. It is impossible to say what its effect will be in twelve or eighteen months without considering the position of Russia. If Russia can hold Germany on land I doubt whether Germany will stand twelve or eighteen months' continuous, intensified and increased bombing, affecting, as it must, her war production, her power of resistance, her industries and her will to resist (by which I mean morale).*'

Thankfully for the future of Bomber Command, it was the Singleton Report which curried the most favour. Regardless of the debate within the Cabinet, a new document was drawn up by the Air Ministry known as the Area Bombing Directive. Issued on 14 February 1942, its main thrust was that '... the primary objective of your operations should be focused on the morale of the enemy civil population and in particular the industrial workers.' It was no coincidence that ACM Sir Arthur Harris (1892–1984), a determined supporter of strategic bombing, was appointed C-in-C of Bomber Command on 22 February 1942.

Bomber Command's very existence within the Second World War had hung in the balance and, despite this 'boardroom' victory, its bombing policy was destined to be questioned throughout the war and Harris would unfairly bear the brunt of it until his death.

The Pathfinder Concept

Group Captain S. O. Bufton (1908–1993)

Sidney Osborne Bufton is often overlooked in RAF history; his significant role in forming the concept of a target marking force, laid the foundation blocks for a permanent unit. Bufton joined the RAF in 1927 and began his flying training with 4 FTS (Flying Training School) the following year. He served as a pilot with 100 Squadron, before becoming a QFI with 5 FTS at Sealand, Flintshire. Before the outbreak of the war, Bufton served in many roles with the RAF, gaining valuable experience. Now a wing commander, he became the CO of 10 Squadron at Leeming, flying the Whitley, in July 1940. By March the following year, he was posted to command 76 Squadron which became only the second unit to introduce the Halifax into front-line service. This was followed by a short tenure as the station commander of Pocklington, Yorkshire, before being posted on 14 November 1941, to become Deputy Director of Bomber Operations.

This important role now put Bufton in a powerful position to put his own opinions forward to senior Air Ministry staff. His first and, probably, most significant task was to bring to the Ministry's attention the need for a Target Finding Force. The Luftwaffe had been using its Knickenbein radio navigational aid to accurately attack British targets but they still found the need for a small, special force of 'fire-raisers'. Thus, Kampfgruppe 100 was born in November 1939, equipped with the Heinkel He111H. This 'Pathfinder' unit would simply fly ahead of the main force and mark the target with IBs (incendiary bombs). This method was used by the Germans to devastating effect against Coventry, Liverpool, Plymouth and London.

Bufton had great foresight and, more importantly, courage to approach senior staff with the idea of an 'elite' force, consisting of at least six squadrons acting as target finders for the main force. Modelling the concept on Kg100, the idea was not well received by the Bomber Command C-in-C at the time, AVM J. E. A. Baldwin, or any of the group commanders. There is no doubt that even if the idea was thought of favourably, the idea of an 'elite' force would have been frowned upon by all. Elitism was not encouraged in all military environments and in particular the air force of the day, who thought the idea would have a major impact on the regular squadrons. Bufton thought it would have the opposite effect and the new force would be something to aspire to.

Baldwin rejected the idea, but this did not stop an even more determined Bufton from approaching the new C-in-C, Sir Arthur Harris, in March 1942. Once again,

'He was a man who would not accept second best; success on one day was only a springboard for greater success on the next day. He was restless, imaginative, and receptive to new ideas from his subordinates. All who served under him knew that he would never ask anyone to do anything he would not have been prepared to do himself – the hallmark of a true leader. One pilot who served with him wrote, "The loyalty shown to him by 8 Group was derived mainly from his example and in the knowledge that anything we would do, he could do better".' The words of Air Marshal Sir Ivor Broom DSO DFC AFC about AVM Don Bennett who is pictured here supporting 'his' 8 Group airmen. (via Author)

though, Harris and all the group commanders were unanimously against the new force. However, they were not stubborn enough to ignore the fact that something needed to be done. In fact, 5 Group in particular were developing their own target marking techniques and it was suggested that all groups should train at least one squadron in a similar fashion.

It was events on a grander scale that gave Bufton the break he needed. The very existence of Bomber Command was still under the spotlight and with the Admiralty and Army gaining more political favour than the RAF, Bufton's idea was grasped from a higher level. Well aware of Bufton's proposal, the Chief of Air Staff, ACM Portal overruled Harris and all the group commanders and ordered that a new Target Finding Force be established as soon as possible.

The new Pathfinder Force was now in the hands of Harris and his wise choice of Don Bennett as its commander was ideal. Bufton's tenacity and the constant pressure on Harris to bring Bomber Command out of the doldrums paid off. Bufton was not popular during his tour at the Air Ministry, especially with the C-in-C who disliked bureaucratic interference and considered Bufton to be his prime antagonist. However, in March 1943, Bufton was promoted to Air Commodore and became the Director of Bomber Operations until 1945 when he gained his own group in the Middle East. A variety of postings followed until he retired on 17 October 1961, having served as the Assistant Chief of Staff (Intelligence) in the rank of AVM. His main achievement will always be his role in establishing the Pathfinder Force and this great man should be more credited for doing so.

Early Beginnings and Formation

The first 8 Group was formed on 1 April 1918 at No.1 Cumberland Place, Southampton, to control No.2 Area under the command of Brig-Gen J. M. Steel. The group was renamed the South Western Area from 8 May 1918. This tasking was short as, on 8 August, it was renamed No.8 (Training) Group and was

8 Group, Headquarter's official crest with the motto 'We Guide to Strike'. The group existed in its third and final form from January 1943 to December 1945. (via Author)

disbanded on 15 May 1919, its responsibilities being transferred to 7 Group.

The group was reformed on 9 September 1941 as No.8 (Light Day Bomber) Group at Brampton Grange, Huntingdonshire, under the command of Air Cdre F. J. Fogarty. He was superseded by AVM D. F. Stevensen in December 1941. However, a re-organisation saw 8 Group disband once again on 28 January 1942, Brampton Grange being taken over by the USAAF.

Reformation took place again on 15 August 1942 as the Pathfinder Force at Wyton but operating within the constraints of 3 Group Bomber Command under the command of Air Cdre D. C. T. Bennett. It was not until 8 January 1943 that the group was officially reformed as No.8 (Pathfinder Force) Group, now under the command of Bennett who, by the end of the year, was an acting AVM. The group moved to Castle Hill House, Huntingdon on 15 May 1943 and remained there until it was disbanded on 15 December 1945. Prior to this, Bennett relinquished command to AVM J. R. Whitley on 21 May 1945.

Despite having been disbanded eight years previously, the group's badge was officially authorised on 11 March 1953, proudly displaying the motto 'We Guide to Strike'.

Operations

1942

August 1942 – A tentative start

The first Pathfinder-led operation took place on 18/19 August 1942 against the port of Flensburg on the Baltic coast. Despite having formed only three days earlier, the new PFF was able to contribute 31 aircraft in this historic raid for the new PFF. A total of 31 crews from 7, 35, 83 and 156 Squadrons took part in the raid and competition was fierce to become the first Pathfinder aircraft to cross the enemy coast. The prize went to Flt Lt D. R. Greenup and his crew in their 156 Squadron Wellington, from Warboys.

Being on the coast, Flensburg should have been a relatively straightforward target but the weather dictated otherwise. Strong winds which had not been forecast by the Met men pushed the force of 118 aircraft north of the target along the Danish coast. This area, with its many inlets, gave the (wrong) impression of being very similar to the Flensburg area and 16 Pathfinder crews claimed to have marked the target. This marking was then bombed by 78 aircraft from the main force. Unfortunately, the target marked was, in fact, the Danish towns of Sønderborg and Abenra which were both hit, along with a large area of countryside. Twenty-six houses were destroyed, 660 damaged but only four Danish people were killed.

This was not an auspicious start for the force and its critics reared their heads, stating that Bomber Command operations back in 1940 were more accurate than this attack. In defence of the Pathfinders, the poorly forecast weather conditions made success an impossible task. To add insult to injury, 35 Squadron became the first PFF unit to lose an aircraft when Sgt J. W. Smith in Halifax II W1226 was shot down by enemy fighters half a mile east-south-east of Sønderborg at Ladegården Farm. The Halifax was actually attacked by a pair of Messerschmitt Bf110 night-fighters from 5/NJG3, one of which was claimed as shot down. A second Bf110, being flown by Fw Herbert Altner, sent several shells into the fuselage which started a fire at approximately 0008 hrs. All the crew managed to escape the crippled aircraft, only to be arrested by Danish police and handed over to the Wehrmacht to become POWs for the rest of the war.

Frankfurt on 24/25 August was selected as the second Pathfinder operation but, like Flensburg, the marking force had difficulty finding the target in the cloudy conditions. The force of 226 aircraft, the majority of which were Wellingtons, dropped most of their bombs in open country to the north-west of the city. However, local reports did state that some bombs fell within the city, causing minimal damage.

As if to rub salt into the wound, and I'm sure it was not deliberate, a small 5 Group operation involving just three Lancasters and three targets took place ahead and on the same route as the main Frankfurt attack. The towns of Bingen, Mayen and the home of the Western Army Headquarters at Bad Kreiznach were successfully attacked without loss. The AOC 5 Group, ACM Sir Alec Coryton KCB, KBE, MVO, DFC was still seething about losing his best unit, 83 Squadron, to the PFF and this possible resentment of the new group brought about a new level of competiveness from 5 Group who would continue to prove its own point, that it was the best group in Bomber Command.

The Pathfinders were praised by Bomber Command Headquarters for their precision marking over Nuremberg on the night of 28/29 August. The force was ordered to attack from as low as possible and this was probably the main reason for the PFF accuracy. On this night the Pathfinders used 'Red Blobs' for the first time, giving the main force an excellent indication of the A/P (Aiming Point). As the name suggests, the new TI (Target Indicator) burned bright red because of a mix of rubber, benzol and phosphorous, all contained within a converted 250 lb bomb casing.

The PFF lost another five aircraft on the Nuremberg raid although, of the two 7 Squadron Stirlings lost, both crash-landed without loss away from their home bases. The first month of PFF operations had achieved mixed results from the 175 sorties flown but it was obviously early days and techniques needed to be fine-tuned while new ones were being developed behind the scenes. The loss rate, which equated to 9% of the PFF squadrons and 15 aircraft lost, did nothing to help recruit volunteers.

One of those new techniques which would change not only PFF operations but Bomber Command tactics as a whole was being developed by 109 Squadron who had moved to Wyton on 6 August 1942. It would be several months before their efforts would be rewarded.

September 1942 – Illuminating, marking/route-marking and backing-up

The month did not start well, with the very reason for the PFF's existence being questioned by Harris himself. The target was Saarbrücken, capital of the Saarland, located just over the French/German border. A mixed bunch of 231 bombers set out on this attack and all seemed well as the PFF markers were placed on what they thought was the middle of the town, followed by 205 bombers accurately bombing on the flares. The PFF had actually 'accurately' marked the smaller industrial town of Saarlouis, 13 miles to the north-west. The town and several surrounding villages were heavily bombed and, despite not a single bomb dropping on the intended target, the industrial damage caused to Saarlouis meant that the raid was not a failure. Success the following night over Karlsruhe was welcomed and on 4/5 September the opportunity for Bennett's men to explore new techniques was taken over Bremen.

A force of 251 aircraft approached Bremen, once again led by the PFF who split themselves up into three smaller groups. The first, named 'illuminators', lit up the target area using white flares, the second, the 'visual backers' dropped coloured flares, called PVMs (Primary Visual Markers) onto the A/P, and the third group, called the 'backers-up', dropped their all-incendiary bomb loads onto the coloured flares. This system of illuminating, marking and backing up would form the basis for all PFF operations for the duration of the Second World War. The raid was a total success and the PFF suffered no losses.

Düsseldorf, on the night of 10/11 September, played host to another new marking device. The PVMs used were called 'Pink Pansies' which were filled with the same ingredients as the Red Blob but with a different colour and considerably larger in size. The Pink Pansy used the casing from a 4,000 lb bomb although its actual weight was nearer to 2,800 lb. Coloured flares were also used on this night to guide a force of 479 aircraft towards the target. The Pink Pansy or PVM was dropped on the A/P while red flares were dropped on the western side of the town and greens on the east. The force simply flew between the red and greens and dropped on the bright pink PVM. The target was marked accurately and the bombing tore out the heart of Düsseldorf. Flak and fighters claimed 33 aircraft out of the main force, sixteen of them from three training groups which made up a large proportion of the Wellingtons, Whitleys and Hampdens that took part. Two 7 Squadron Stirlings and a single 83 Squadron Lancaster failed to return from the PFF contribution.

The Pink Pansy played its part again when the PFF returned to Bremen on 13/14 September. Two Pink Pansies started a large fire of which the large main force of 446 aircraft was exploited. One of them was later seen on a target photograph exploding directly on the aiming point. The force was made up of several Wellingtons from various OTUs (Operational Training Unit) and, out of the 21 aircraft, fifteen of them were Wellingtons. Two of these were from 156 Squadron with the loss of all eleven crew onboard. The PFF accuracy continued the following night against

Wilhelmshaven, resulting in the worst raid reported on this port since the beginning of the war.

The raid on Essen, on 16/17 September, appeared to be a success to the crews bombing overhead as a large explosion, followed by several raging fires, seemed to tear through the city. However, PRU photography the following day revealed very little damage. Although the bombing was scattered, it was still Bomber Command's most successful attack on what was now being nicknamed the 'elusive' Essen by crews.

Two targets were selected for an attack by Bomber Command on the night of 19/20 September 1942. A total of 118 aircraft were detailed for Saarbrücken and another 68 Lancasters and Stirlings would attack Munich. It was the first time that the PFF led two separate attacks simultaneously and, on the Munich operation, it was also the first time route-marking was used. A turning point was selected near to the target which, on this occasion, was the 18-square-mile Ammer See, just over 20 miles west-south-west of Munich. A PFF aircraft dropped a coloured flare near to the lake and from that point the main force made an accurate DR (Dead Reckoning) direct to the centre of Munich which was also lit up by flares. This simple but innovative technique ensured that the bombers were on track at the beginning of the bombing run. While a local report from the Munich authorities is unavailable, crews reported seeing at least one large explosion and the last aircraft over the target also reported 17 fires burning strongly.

In contrast, the Saarbrücken raid was hampered by ground haze and the PFF crews found it difficult to accurately mark the target. Bombing was scattered and, additionally, it was an expensive night for the PFF. In particular, 35 Squadron lost its popular CO (Commanding Officer), Wg Cdr J. H. Marks DSO, DFC, and a very experienced crew. His aircraft, Halifax II W7657 was shot down by a Me110, crashing at Blesme, just over seven miles east of Vitry-le-Francois. Marks, Flt Lt A. J. Child DFC and Plt Off R. L. Leith-Hay-Clark all perished but three of the crew managed to bail out to become POWs.

Sqn Ldr A. Ashworth, in his 156 Squadron Wellington, ordered his crew to abandon the aircraft when his cargo of flares caught fire en route to the target. With smoke pouring through the floor of the Wellington, Ashworth made sure all of his crew were out when he reached for his parachute. To his astonishment, it was not there, so he quickly steered the smoking bomber towards open country and a place to crash land. While doing this, the smoke dissipated and the fire appeared to have extinguished itself. Ashworth continued on to England on his own, making a safe landing at West Malling, Kent.

The remainder of September was devoid of any PFF operations due to poor weather conditions although Bomber Command still attempted to attack several targets. The weather would hamper the PFF for the remainder of the year.

The Pathfinders gained their own Mosquito training unit at Marham on 29 September in the shape of the Mosquito Conversion Unit (MCU), making use of Downham Market as a satellite airfield. The unit was first formed at Horsham St Faith operating the Mosquito T.III, IV and at least one Blenheim IV.

The MCU was renamed 1655 Mosquito Training Unit (MTU) from 18 October in 2 Group to train crews for Mosquito squadrons, with an establishment of nine Mosquito IVs and six Blenheim IV and Vs. No.1655 MCU was absorbed by 13 OTU on 1 May 1943 but reclaimed back by Bomber Command on 1 June 1943, when 13 OTU was transferred to 70 Group control within the new 2nd TAF (Tactical Air Force).

Wg Cdr J. H. Marks DSO, DFC, the popular CO of 35 Squadron was lost, along with his crew, in Halifax II W7657 on 19/20 September 1942. (via Author)

The unit was reformed the same day as 1655 MTU at Finmere (satellite at Bicester) in 2 Group with the same tasking. On 1 July the unit returned to Marham and transferred to 8 Group using Warboys as a satellite airfield although it is probable that Downham Market played a role as well. By this stage the unit strength had swelled to 31 Mosquitoes. On 7 March 1944, the unit moved again, this time to Warboys as its main base, with a flight on detachment at Wyton from 27 June to 30 December. The unit continued to grow, recording a unit strength in June 1944 of 37 Mosquito IV, XVI and XXs, eleven T.3s and 24 Oxfords.

Finally the unit moved to Upper Heyford on 30 December 1944, being absorbed by 16 OTU the following day after 8 Group had relinquished control.

October 1942 – Italian targets

The first operation of the month was a PFF-led attack on Krefeld on 2/3 October but it was not a success. The PFF found dense haze over the target and late marking resulted in the 188-strong force causing little damage.

Heavy thunderstorms all over Britain did not deter Bomber Command from launching a 257-strong attack on Aachen on 5/6 October. However, the severe conditions were claiming victims even as they set out. No.156 Squadron suffered the most, with only five out of the twelve aircraft detailed becoming airborne.

Osnabrück was accurately route-marked and then bombed on 6/7 October without loss to the PFF. But poor weather conditions kept most of Bomber Command on the ground until the night of 13/14 October when the target was Kiel. Much of the bombing that night was successfully drawn away from the city by an effective decoy fire but this did not stop considerable damage being caused in the centre by those who managed to bomb the PFF markers. Once again a strong decoy fire managed to draw away the main force over Cologne on 15/16 October. This, coupled with un-forecast winds, made the PFF's task to mark the centre of Cologne virtually impossible.

A pristine line of 35 Squadron Halifaxes during an inspection at Graveley in October 1942. The squadron operated the Halifax until January 1944, the last in 8 Group to do so. (via Author)

The PFF crews enjoyed a short but welcome break from operations while Bomber Command prepared its forces for a set of new targets. On the night of 22/23 October, Bomber Command recommenced its bombing campaign against Italian targets, the first of eleven operations which would continue until early December. A force of 112 Lancasters of 5 Group and the PFF set out on a clear moonlit night for Genoa and, on arrival, the PFF marking was described as 'prompt and accurate'. Local reports describe heavy damage in the city centre and eastern districts, all without a single aircraft being lost. The following night, a slightly larger force of 122 aircraft returned to Genoa but this time the target was totally cloud-covered. The force did bomb but it was later reported that it had actually hit the town of Savona, 30 miles west of the target along the coast. Three bombers were lost, none of them from the PFF. Milan, on 24/25 October, was visited by 71 aircraft from 1 Group, 3 Group and the PFF but storms en route scattered the small force. Some aircraft strayed over Switzerland and all received a polite warning shot from anti-aircraft fire. Only 39 managed to reach and bomb Milan but local reports do not confirm if much damage was caused.

November 1942 – *Boozer*

Only minor operations were carried out for the remainder of October and it was not until 6/7 November that the PFF were back in the air in force. Two operations were flown: the first was a return to Genoa with 5 Group and a force of 72 Lancasters. The raid appears to have been successful, with good marking by the Lancasters of 83 Squadron. However, the squadron took the brunt of that night's losses with two Lancasters brought down over or near the target and a third within moments of touching down back in England. The second operation that night involved the Stirlings of 7 Squadron, leading a force of 65 aircraft mine-laying from Lorient to the Frisians. Four aircraft were lost on this operation, including Plt Off D. J. Totteman RNZAF and his crew in Stirling I W7620, shot down by Kreigsmarine flak off Vlieland.

It was Genoa again, on 7/8 November, which received a larger force of 175 bombers. This was the most successful of all attacks on this coastal city during the current campaign. The PFF marking was excellent and was described by crews as being 'so well lit you could actually see the buildings topple'. On the down side, ten aircraft were lost; six of these were over England through mid-air collision or running out of fuel. Only one PFF aircraft and its crew were lost, Wellington III X3422, flown by Plt Off D. G. Chell.

A change of tack by Bomber Command on 9/10 November resulted in a return to Germany. A mixed force of 213 aircraft were assembled for an attack on Hamburg, which would turn out to be a complete disaster. For the PFF the raid started going wrong from the outset; 7 Squadron in particular suffering the most. Of the ten Stirlings it dispatched, five returned early because of severe icing and three more were destined not to return to Oakington.

A return to Genoa saw 7 Squadron make use of *Boozer* for the first time on 13/14 November. The device was a rear-facing aerial fitted in the tail of the aircraft, connected to a warning indicator in the wireless operator's compartment. A red light would illuminate when the aircraft was being monitored by Würzburg radar or the AI (Airborne Interception) radar from a night-fighter. It was not officially brought into full operational service until 1943, by which time an additional warning light, generally yellow, would illuminate as well, to indicate searchlights or flak guns vectoring in on the bomber. Nine PFF Stirlings led a 5 Group force of 67 Lancasters against Genoa with great accuracy and no losses. The following night Genoa was attacked again with great accuracy and without loss. Attention was turned to Turin on 18/19 November and, once again, a force of 77 aircraft bombed the target accurately, starting many fires in the city centre. No aircraft were lost this night but six aircrew did not arrive back at Graveley as expected. Whilst returning from the target over the Alps, the 35 Squadron Halifax II DT488, being flown by Sqn Ldr B. V. Robinson caught fire, when a bundle of flares hung-up in the bomb bay ignited. Well aflame, Robinson ordered his crew to bail out but, once they had done so, a rush of air from an open escape hatch extinguished the flames. Robinson flew on alone, eventually landing safely at an airfield in the south of England while his crew became POWs for the remainder of the war. Turin was hit again by the largest raid so far during the current Italian campaign. A total of 232 bombers caused further damage on 20/21 November at the expense of three aircraft, none of them from the PFF.

A return to a German target took place on 22/23 November; this time, Stuttgart. A force of 222 aircraft, led by 25 from the PFF, began the operation with a change of tactics. Rather than forming up at high-altitude, the route to the target was flown at low-level in a successful attempt to outwit the enemy's RDF (Radar Direction Finding) and GCI (Ground Controlled Interception). Flying at no more than 200 ft presented the aircraft's gunners with a multitude of ground targets which normally would be out of range. Low over France, several searchlights, gun posts, trains and even a flak ship were all put out of action during the run in. One particular 83 Squadron Lancaster, flown by Flt Lt P. A. Mackenzie, was one of many en route that enjoyed strafing success. His gunners, Flt Sgt L. Fieldhouse and Sgt C. M. Coghill, set at least one warehouse on fire, shot up two trains and a pair of flak guns. Whilst flying at 200 ft, the enemy still managed to get a pair of searchlights on the Lancaster but, as a trio of flak guns opened up, Fieldhouse and Coghill swiftly silenced them along with the lights. On arrival at the target, despite a bright moon,

One of thousands of 4,000 lb 'Cookies', awaiting delivery to Germany in late 1942 at Wyton. Beyond, is Lancaster I L7540 'U' of 83 Squadron. (www.ww2images.com)

a thin layer of cloud combined with haze made marking the target difficult. Considerable damage did develop in the south-west of the city, mainly in residential areas. Ten aircraft failed to return, including an 83 Squadron Lancaster and a 156 Squadron Wellington, the only consolation being that eight out of the twelve aircrew survived to become POWs.

After three months of continuous operations, Gp Capt D. C. T. Bennett arranged a meeting at Wyton for the COs of 1, 3, 4 and 5 Groups to attend on 28 November. Bennett wanted to hear for himself how the PFF was performing and how it could be improved. The meeting was fairly predictable with 5 Group's AOC, Air Cdre A.

Coryton making suggestions that went against what the other four groups had put forward. The AOCs of 1, 3 and 4 Groups comments were all generally complimentary, only asking for less illumination and more ground-marking. Coryton asked for the exact opposite, Bennett being aware that he was still seething under the surface since losing 'his' 83 Squadron to the new PFF. All present that day did agree that flares were bursting too high which caused the bombers above to be silhouetted, making them easy prey for flak and visible to night-fighters. It was decided that barometric fuses would solve the problem of the flares bursting too high and the proposal was immediately forwarded to HQ Bomber Command who had no objection. The idea of route-marking and land-marking was also discussed and all groups agreed that this worked well and should continue. Coryton said nothing, so this was interpreted as his only positive comment of the meeting. No. 5 Group would have their day and 83 Squadron back, but Coryton was destined never to see it while he was in command.

On 28/29 November, 228 aircraft set out for Turin again and, despite 67 aircraft bombing before the PFF started marking, the city was severely hit. No.5 Group stole the show when Wg Cdr G. Gibson and Flt Lt W. N. Whamond dropped 8,000 lb bombs for the first time on an Italian target. It was Turin again the following night, but a much smaller force of 29 Stirlings and seven Lancasters of 3 Group were led by sixteen PFF aircraft. Poor weather prevented all but eighteen aircraft crossing the Alps, fourteen of them from the PFF. All claimed to have bombed Turin but little damage was reported locally. Three Stirlings were lost this night, including 7 Squadron's R9150 being flown by Flt Lt R. M. Smith DFC. Five perished, including Smith, but two managed to escape the bomber which was shot down by a night-fighter near Pecy in southern France.

December 1942 – *OBOE* trials & *Wanganui* into service

The month did not start well because of thick haze over Frankfurt on 2/3 December. Unable to locate the city, the force of 112 aircraft were distracted by a decoy fire and much of the bombing fell in open country. The PFF escaped without loss but two 7 Squadron Stirlings had close shaves with Ju88 night-fighters, resulting in one being shot down by mid-upper gunner Fg Off I. C. Meickle.

The weather dictated success or failure over Manheim on 6/7 December. Some 9/10ths cloud over the target meant that the PFF saw no point in dropping their flares and the force of 272 aircraft relied on DR to bomb the target. Wherever the bombs fell that night, they did not cause much damage to Manheim and only 500 IBs were reported to have dropped on the city.

It was back to Italy on 8/9 December, with Turin being on the receiving end of an attack by 133 aircraft of 5 Group and the PFF. Despite the rivalry, the combination worked well, with excellent marking by the PFF, followed by equally accurate bombing by the 5 Group Lancasters. At least one 8,000 lb bomb fell between the railway yards and the river causing a fire which could be seen 60 miles away. The last wave of attacks on Italian targets came to an end on 11/12 December when Turin was singled out again. It was a raid that never should have taken place, with continuous cloud en route and icing which caused half of the 82 aircraft dispatched to return home early. Only 28 crews managed to cross the Alps and claimed to have bombed Turin which only reported three HE bombs falling on the city, with two of them failing to detonate.

A bright moonlit night, combined with good visibility over Duisburg on 20/21 December, broke a period of inactivity for Bomber Command. Flares were dropped to the north and south of the town and the main force of 232 aircraft claimed to have bombed accurately although local reports do not confirm or deny. Night-fighters were in abundance and twelve aircraft failed to return, three of them from the PFF.

The same night, 109 Squadron, who had been flying continually with the Mosquito since August 1942 trying to perfect the *Oboe* blind bombing system, flew against the enemy for the first time. The target was a power station at Lutterade, a small Dutch town close to the German border. The trial, the first of many, was flown by six Mosquitoes led by Sqn Ldr H. E. Bufton (brother of Sidney) and his navigator Flt Lt E. L. I. Fould. On approaching the target, it was Bufton who dropped the first *Oboe*-aimed bombs, along with two other crews from the small formation. The *Oboe* transmitter in the remaining three aircraft failed to work properly and they bombed elsewhere, a familiar story to those who had been working on the project for many months. Post-attack reconnaissance flown the following day over Lutterade was unable to establish whether the *Oboe* attack had been successful because of craters from a previous raid. However, local reports stated that nine bombs fell in open country, approximately a mile from the power station, very close to a large area of housing.

The last major raid of 1942 took place against Munich on 21/22 December. A force of 137 aircraft of 1 and 5 Groups and the PFF set course on a clear night, conditions which were favourable for the enemy night-fighter. On the outward flight, several aircraft were engaged and some succumbed to the night-fighter guns. On arrival at the last turning point at the Wurm See, the clear night changed into 10/10ths cloud so the bombing had to take place using a DR run. A total of 110 bombers claimed to have bombed the city but the vast majority was once again distracted by a decoy fire and the ordnance fell in open fields. It was not an auspicious end to the year as another twelve bombers failed to return.

For the PFF, the remainder of the year was taken up with small *Oboe* operations flown by a handful of Mosquitoes. Operations included sorties to Hamborn, Rheinhausen, Medrich and Essen. The latter, on 23/24 December, involving five Mosquitoes, one of which managed to hit the main Krupps armament factory in Essen. This was repeated on the night of Christmas Eve and on 29/30 December proving that *Oboe* could work. Eight Lancasters of 83 Squadron took part in the *Oboe* trial for the first time on 31 December/1 January 1943 on Düsseldorf. The small operation was led by a pair of *Oboe* Mosquitoes, one flown by Sqn Ldr Bufton dropping Skymarker flares, effectively performing the first *Wanganui* of the war. The Lancaster crews were ordered to bomb when they had a flare in their sights. Local reports show nine different bombing incidents, of which six were industrial, although no serious damage was caused. The same night, three more *Oboe*-equipped Mosquitoes attacked the night-fighter control building at Florennes airfield in Belgium with six HE (High Explosive) bombs from 28,000 ft. The attack which took place through solid cloud was inconclusive.

The PFF had flown 1,091 sorties since its formation. This had come at a cost, with 50 crews lost over enemy territory. As mentioned earlier, the role of the Wellington and Stirling was being brought into question. Out of the 54 aircraft lost so far by the PFF, twenty were Wellingtons and eighteen were Stirlings, compared to ten Lancasters and six Halifaxes. While the end for the Wellington was in sight, the Stirlings of 7 Squadron would plough on for another eight months and pay the price as a result. Bennett's dream of an all Lancaster and Mosquito force was still a long way away.

2

Operations

1943

January 1943 – 8 Group is born, new TIs, ground markers & H2S operational

The year began much as it had ended, with a continuous stream of *Oboe*-equipped Mosquitoes leading increasingly larger formations of Lancasters. Essen was attacked seven more times during the month. The largest and last *Oboe* trial on 13/14 January involved 66 Lancasters and three Mosquitoes. The results were mixed during all the trials flown but it was clear that *Oboe* was here to stay for the remainder of the war. One interesting tactic of the German night-fighters on 13/14 January was the use of decoy flares to try and distract the bombers away from the sky-marking. It did not work on this occasion but it did show that the enemy was quite aware of the tactics being employed by Bomber Command.

The first big raid of the year did not take place until 14/15 January and, compared to operations over Germany, this was a 'milk-run' for the PFF. The target was the U-boat base at Lorient on the French coast. A total of 122 aircraft took part, including nine Wellingtons and six Halifaxes from 6 (RCAF) Group on their first bombing operation. The following night, another 157 aircraft approached Lorient to find it covered in 3-5/10th drifting cloud but, showing great discipline, the force did not attack until a decent break opened up. The bombing was much more accurate on this occasion with at least 800 buildings destroyed. The majority of the population had wisely already evacuated after the previous night's attack resulting in just twelve civilians killed.

Berlin, on 16/17 January, was the first time that the PFF led a raid on this unpopular but important target. The German capital had not been attacked for fourteen months and expectations were high. The 201 Lancasters and Halifaxes involved in this raid made it the first all four-engined operation of the war. The raid did not start well and thick cloud almost all the way did not help navigation. The cloud cleared on approach to the city but it was still covered in haze. The PFF were using proper red TIs for the first time but were still unable to effectively mark the target. Beyond the range of *Gee*, navigation would eventually be improved when the range of *Oboe* could be extended. The following night, another 187 aircraft set out for Berlin in improved weather conditions but the PFF were once again unable to mark the centre of the city. It was a surprising tactic by Bomber Command to fly to the same target on consecutive nights and even more surprising that they would fly the same route. As a result, the German night-fighters were waiting and nineteen Lancasters and three Halifaxes were lost, equating to 11.8% of the force. No further attacks on Berlin would take place using target indicators until H2S became available.

A pair of *Oboe*-equipped Mosquitoes showed how aircraft fitted with the latest modern aids could inflict almost as much damage as a larger force. On 22/23 January, the Mosquitoes set out for Cologne to carry out the first *Oboe* attack on the city. These two machines managed to damage 55 houses, kill five people and injure another 22. While these are still small numbers, only two years previously, a force ten times the size was lucky to find Cologne let alone plant bombs accurately in the middle of it.

The PFF, up until now, was controlled via 3 Group because it was not a group in its own right. But, on 25 January, (backdated to 13 January), the status of the PFF was raised, to the independent 8 Group. This meant an increase in staff and all orders were received direct from Bomber Command rather than from 3 Group. Bennett was promoted to Air Commodore but the Air Staff still wanted to place an AVM above him. Harris stuck to his promise of keeping Bennett in charge, much to the annoyance of the Air Staff, who wanted to keep a tighter rein on him. Bennett's first task was to rid 156 Squadron of its Wellingtons in favour of the Lancaster. A maintenance depot was then set up at Wyton, specifically for 8 Group's Lancasters. A similar one was set up for the Mosquito at Upwood later in the war.

Düsseldorf, on 27/28 January, was another ground-breaking raid for 8 Group. It was 109 Squadron's first chance to shine in front of a decent-sized force of 162 aircraft rather than the smaller experimental raids. It was also the first time that the *Oboe*-equipped Mosquitoes carried out ground-marking. These markers were now standard TIs which were designed to burst and cascade just a few feet above the ground rather than the less accurate parachuted sky-markers. On arrival over the target, three of the five Mosquitoes involved dropped red TIs, backed up by thirteen Lancasters, eleven of which dropped green TIs. Despite the target being covered by a thin 10/10th layer of low stratus cloud, the 157 bombers of the main force could still see the TIs glowing bright, and all bombed on them. All of those who bombed this night said they would not have attacked without the help of 8 Group.

Another milestone during this month was the first H2S attack of the war. It was

8 Group's Stirlings and Halifaxes that were fitted with the device on a raid to Hamburg on 30/31 January. The force of 148 aircraft was also treated to some colourful and accurate marking en route and on the target. Red flares were dropped as route markers and, approximately 16 miles from the target, these changed to green. The H2S equipped aircraft ground-marked the centre of Hamburg with red TIs backed up by greens. A second wave of marking dropped further TIs which were red with green stars as a precaution in case the target was cloud covered. Despite the new equipment, the bombing by 130 aircraft was scattered and post-attack reconnaissance found very little new damage. It is thought that, despite 315 tons of bombs being dropped, the vast majority of them fell in the river Elbe and surrounding marshes. H2S would become more effective in the future.

It had been a remarkable month for the new 8 Group. It was maturing fast, gaining new aircraft and new techniques which it was rapidly honing. Receiving group status had also given the Pathfinders a new respect and, with its newly-promoted leader, it could only go from strength to strength.

February 1943 – Blind-bombing success and FIDO (Fog Investigation Dispersal Operation)

A busy month lay ahead for 8 Group as unseasonal good weather dominated February. It was, however, a cloudy night on 2/3 February when 161 aircraft set course for Cologne, led by a pair of *Oboe* Mosquitoes and 7 Squadron's H2S-equipped Stirlings. Because of the cloud, markers were dropped by all of 8 Group's aircraft but, like Hamburg before it, the results were not as expected. The city was certainly hit by a number of bombs but these were scattered and no significant industrial targets were hit. Five bombers failed to return. Most significant was 7 Squadron Stirling I R9264 being flown by Sqn Ldr W. A. Smith DFC MID. The bomber was shot down by a night-fighter of I.NJG/1 and crashed at Hendrik-Ido-Ambacht in Holland, killing Smith and four other aircrew; only the mid-upper and rear-gunners managed to escape the stricken aircraft. Despite being damaged, the Germans had gained themselves a good example of an H2S set. Quickly repaired by the German company Telefunken, it was tested, giving the enemy the information they needed to develop a system later known as 'Naxos' which, fitted in a night-fighter, could home in on any aircraft carrying H2S. This was quite a blow for Bomber Command which had waited so long for it to enter service, only for it to fall into enemy hands after just two operational sorties.

A larger force of 263 aircraft returned to Hamburg on 3/4 February but severe icing conditions outbound over the North Sea caused many to return home early.

Once again, despite having the assistance of H2S, the PFF were unable to deliver accurate concentrated marking. Bombing was scattered again and the German night-fighters made it a miserable night for Bomber Command. Sixteen bombers were shot down. The PFF were lucky; only 35 Squadron Halifax II W7923 was written off after it crash landed at Graveley because of flak damage. There were several close calls with night-fighters, including one involving 156 Squadron Lancaster flown by Plt Off V. S. Moore. Whilst flying straight and level so his navigator could take an astro-fix and his wireless operator a loop bearing, the Lancaster was suddenly attacked from below. The aircraft was raked from nose to tail, wounding the bomb aimer in the foot but, luckily, no one else and the bomber seemed to keep on flying. The aircraft was still carrying its load of TIs and, as the Lancaster

twisted and turned, the load was jettisoned. As the flares burned brightly, the night-fighter broke off its attack, probably thinking the Lancaster was on fire, leaving it to limp home back to Warboys. The starboard inner engine had been knocked out in the attack and, after extinguishing a fire, the bomber settled down for the flight home. Moore carried a good landing and the crew survived to fight another day.

The now deserted Lorient was revisited on 7/8 February by 323 bombers. The PFF plan worked perfectly, with illuminators being accurately dropped which enabled the visual markers to identify the aiming point and ground mark it. A poor decoy fire on the edge of the town did not detract the main force from delivering a devastating two wave attack on Lorient. A larger force of 466 aircraft returned to Lorient on 13/14 February, dropping over 1,000 tons of bombs on the already ruined town. While further damage was caused, it was not as accurate as the previous raid and, unlike the first, the PFF lost another Halifax from 35 Squadron. Lorient was attacked for a third time on 16/17 February. The U-boat pens still defiantly stood intact and operational while the rest of the town suffered another 377-strong bomber raid. Over the past three raids, 1,675 aircraft claimed to have bombed the target, dropping nearly 4,000 tons of bombs. It was clear that the pens could not be destroyed from the air but the surrounding communication lines were constantly attacked so as to disrupt supplies reaching the U-boats. Lorient was never captured from the Germans and it did not surrender until the very end of the Second World War despite being surrounded by an American garrison for months. Today, the pens still stand, without a single bomb scar to show for Bomber Command's efforts.

The H2S blind-bombing device was having difficulty proving itself until the raid on Wilhelmshaven on 11/12 February. The PFF aircraft leading the operation were more prepared than at any other time to deal with whatever weather conditions faced

Handley Page Halifax II Srs IA, HR928 TL–L of 35 Squadron with Sqn Ldr A. P. Cranswick at the controls. (via Author)

Wg Cdr T. G. 'Hamish' Mahaddie with 'erks' (ground crew) of 'A' Flight, 7 Squadron at Oakington. Later promoted to Group Captain, 'Hamish' joined the staff of PFF HQ and quickly became 'a horse thief for the Pathfinders', becoming particularly adept at finding the right kind of men and crews for 8 Group. (via Author)

them this night. A complicated brief for the PFF crews included the following: If the cloud over the target is less than 5/10th then the H2S will drop flares and try and identify the target visually (*Newhaven*); if 5/8ths cloud-cover then the PFF are to ground mark blindly using H2S (*Parramatta*); and finally, if faced with 8/10th or more, the PFF are to drop skymarkers (*Wanganui*) the least reliable of the three. The force of 177 aircraft set course for the north German port only to find the target completely covered in cloud. The PFF set to work dropping sky-markers, keeping the A/P marked for over fifteen minutes. Once again, this was performed with great accuracy and the town was hit very hard. One devastating explosion witnessed by the whole force was the naval ammunition dump at Mariensiel blowing up on the western side of the town. The glow from the explosion kept the sky lit for nearly ten minutes and was visible 60 miles away. This was a great success, not just for the PFF but it also represented the first blind-bombing success by the H2S radar.

The *Oboe*-equipped Mosquitoes of 109 Squadron were beginning to make their presence felt on 15/16 February. Six of them attacked the Krupps factory in Essen, Rheinhausen and the night-fighter airfield at St Trond. These small insurgency-type raids would continue to grow throughout the war and spread themselves over an increasingly diverse array of targets.

Back in November 1942, Bennett had eagerly agreed that a new fog-dispersal device should be tested at one of his airfields. Graveley was chosen to be the first operational airfield to test FIDO on 18 February. The system relied on steel pipes which ran either side of the runway. When fuel was pumped through these and ignited at intervals by burners, the fog would lift. In fact, Bennett flew the first aircraft, possibly an Oxford, landing with a cross wind between the lit burners. The device would go on to save many air crew who would otherwise have had to divert into a strange airfield or even bail out because of lack of fuel.

The next three major raids on German targets, with the exception of a failed attack on Bremen on 21/22 February, were against Wilhelmshaven. None of the three attacks were as successful as the one earlier in the month and, when things went wrong, all fingers were pointed at the Pathfinders. The first, on 18/19 February involved 195 bombers, 35 of them from the PFF. It was a clear night and the force was able to map read its way from the Frisian Islands the last 60 miles to the target. The PFF claimed good marking but despite the vast majority of the main force bombing on them, very little damage was caused. The following night, the same operation was repeated with 338 aircraft but once again, despite the PFF claiming accurate marking, almost all of the bombing fell to the north. After this raid, the most basic error appears to have been made. Unbeknown to 8 Group, they had been issued with out-of-date pre-war maps which did not show any of the recent town developments. The third raid took place on 24/25 February, but the 115 aircraft of

6 and 8 Groups appeared to have made little impact on Wilhelmshaven. Local reports described a 'small raid' with very little damage, the only consolation for Bomber Command was that all returned home safely. Wilhelmshaven was not attacked again until October 1944.

All five PFF squadrons took part in a raid on St Nazaire on the night of 28 February/1 March. St Nazaire, like Lorient, was a major U-boat base from which Allied shipping was being sunk at an alarming rate. Mosquitoes from 109 Squadron led the way, two of the four aircraft involved dropped greens on the A/P and this was backed up by the heavies dropping more flares. The A/P was continually marked for a record-breaking 34 minutes. The raid was a total success with widespread destruction tearing across the town. One airman described the carnage as a 'bubbling mass of red fire'. Local reports state that over 60% of the town was destroyed but fortunately only 29 people were killed, apparently, the population was warned subversively that the raid was coming. Like Lorient, the main objective was the U-boat pens which stood up to the onslaught and continued to operate until late 1944. It, too, remained in German hands until the end of the war.

Both attacks on the U-boat pens were seen by Harris as a complete waste of Bomber Command resources. He was, of course, right and even without the benefit of hindsight it must have been clear to those involved in these operations that these were not the kind of targets they should be attacking in early 1943. Even when larger more penetrating weapons became available they were not wasted on U-boat pens. With H2S and *Oboe* now at his disposal, he quite rightly wanted to concentrate his resources on Germany as the Battle of the Ruhr approached.

March 1943 – The Battle of the Ruhr begins

The month began with a trip to Berlin on 1/2 March and, once again, the PFF led this raid in force. Some 302 aircraft took part, including H2S-equipped Halifaxes and Stirlings, plus sixteen Lancasters from 83 and 156 Squadrons who assisted with the marking. When the force was 100 miles north-west of Berlin, the first of many route-markers were dropped near Bahlenhüsch. These continued until warning flares were dropped 12 miles from the target bringing the main attacking force of 274 aircraft to bear. H2S was still more accurate on a coastal target and the mass of indistinguishable features that made up Berlin did not look clear on the operator's screens. Despite this, the TIs were dropped near the centre of the city and backed-up but the main weight of the raid fell on the south-western side of the city. The bombing quickly spread to an area of 100 square miles and 22 acres' worth of workshops and rail repair shops were destroyed in the Templehof area alone. This was a classic example of a heavy Bomber Command raid that was not particularly accurate but still caused a great deal of collateral damage. One ironic incident occurred when the Telefunken works, where the captured H2S set was being repaired, was hit by several bombs. If the captured set was damaged, it was irrelevant because a second set was gifted intact to the enemy when Sqn Ldr P. C. Elliott DFC and crew in their 35 Squadron Halifax II W7877 were shot down by a night-fighter near Goor in Holland. This was the only PFF aircraft lost on this operation.

The first of 47 sorties which would be known as the 'Battle of the Ruhr' began on 5 March. All but six of these operations were directed at targets in Germany which would continue until 24 July. This new phase of Bomber Command operation was referred to by Sir Arthur Harris as his 'main offensive' and would continue into the spring of 1944. Since taking charge in February 1942, Harris had nurtured and steadily brought his forces up to a strength from where they could consistently dispatch up to 600 bombs per operation. By the end of the Battle of the Ruhr, this had increased to 800 and the average bomb load dropped per night was well over 2,000 tons. Bomber Command also had the added advantage of 8 Group and, in particular, *Oboe* which could now consistently mark any target in the Ruhr with amazing accuracy, certainly compared to the operations being carried out in 1941 and early 1942.

The first target, chosen by Harris himself, was Essen on 5/6 March. He knew the fledgling 8 Group needed a boost and also had to prove that it was proficient to lead Bomber Command into battle. Up to this date, Essen had not been successfully bombed, but the 442 strong force, including 35 PFF aircraft, were determined to change that. The success of the raid depended on eight *Oboe* Mosquitoes but three of them had to return with technical problems. In fact, it looked like Essen was going to escape again because a further 53 aircraft, an unimpressive record for Bomber Command, also had to turn back with various mechanical problems. The remainder continued and, on arrival over the target, which was covered in traditional ground haze, the PFF began their plan. With *Oboe* working effectively in the remaining Mosquitoes, the PFF began a *Musical Parramatta* dropping red TIs while 22 heavies backed-up with reds. Yellow land markers were also dropped 15 miles from the target so that the main force could attack from a datum point to avoid a collision over the target. The centre of Essen was marked perfectly and the timing of the backers-up was excellent, all performed 'blind' thanks to *Oboe*. The main force followed in three waves, the first was all Halifax, the second Wellingtons and Stirlings and the final wave was all Lancasters. IBs were dropped in the first two waves while the Lancasters poured HE onto the intense fires below. The raid lasted for 40 minutes and 362 aircraft claimed to have bombed the target on the night that Bomber Command flew its 100,000th sortie of the war. The raid was an amazing success and post-attack reports recorded over 160 acres of damage. A total of fourteen aircraft were lost, including two Lancasters from 83 and 156 Squadron and their fourteen aircrew. It was almost fifteen aircraft lost, when another 83 Squadron Lancaster was nearly blown out of the sky as the 4,000 lb 'cookie' it had just dropped was hit by flak. The blast from the bomb sent the Lancaster vertically 500 ft, showering the machine with bomb fragments and shrapnel. A small fire was quickly extinguished and the bomb-aimer had the presence of mind to jettison the photo flashes in the bomb bay. On return to Wyton, the souvenir hunters spent the following day removing thousands of pieces of the cookie from the lucky Lancaster, including the bomb's filler plug from the main plane and the arming pistol from an engine nacelle.

Targets beyond the range of *Oboe* were still proving difficult to bomb accurately; Nuremburg on 8/9 March was no exception. With no moon to help, the PFF had to rely on H2S and visual navigation to lead the total force of 335 aircraft to the target. Haze over Nuremburg added to the problems and the red TIs were scattered across the city. The backers-up had to select several options to drop their green TIs and the resulting bombing spread itself along a 10-mile route. Over half of the bombs dropped fell outside the city but those that did not caused considerable damage to several important industrial targets. Local reports state that over 600 buildings were destroyed and another 1,400 damaged, including the Siemens-Schukert electrical works and M.A.N. diesel engine factories.

Despite winds that were not properly forecast, the raid on Munich on 9/10 March was the most effective of the war so far. The use of good route-marking, starting as far away as Metz in France (250 miles west of the target) helped to bring the force of 264 aircraft on track for Munich. The final route-marker was once again dropped near the Ammer See and the remaining 23-mile run to target was flown on DR. The lead PFF aircraft marking was planted into the centre of the haze-covered city and the majority of the raid stretched across the western half of it. While little was made of the raid from the crews involved, the ferocity of intercepted German radio reports was interpreted as another success for Bomber Command.

The effectiveness and accuracy of the first three raids of the Battle of the Ruhr are worthy of note. While all three were successful in their own right, the use of *Oboe* for Essen and H2S plus visual methods for the further Nuremberg and Munich raids shows how human input lessened the accuracy. Add the factor that the *Oboe*-equipped Mosquitoes, up until now, were relatively unmolested by both flak and fighters while those bombers using H2S were an easy target.

Air Vice Marshal Don Bennett presiding over a meeting at Pathfinder HQ while it was still located at Wyton. Bennett was the RAF's youngest Air Vice Marshal. (www.ww2images.com)

Bomber Command's good run came to an end over Stuttgart on 11/12 March. The PFF had skilfully dropped IBs on Baden-Baden en route to act as a beacon so that the main force of 314 aircraft did not stray into the flak over Strasbourg and Karlsruhe. On arrival, the PFF claimed to have marked Stuttgart accurately but the main force lagged behind, giving the Germans their first opportunity of the war to use their own dummy TIs. This must have been successful as most of the bombing fell in open country and only civilian housing was hit. Night-fighters were also prevalent and eleven bombers failed to return, including 83 Squadron's Lancaster I ED313 which was shot down near Sogny-en-l'Angle. The Lancaster was attacked three times by a fighter, having to drop down to 2,500 ft in an effort to escape. It was at this point that five of the crew managed to bail out, only the mid-upper and rear gunner, who may have already been killed in the fighter attack, did not escape.

A period of rest followed the Stuttgart raid and it was not until 22/23 March that the PFF were in action again. The target was St Nazaire and, despite 3 Group recalling its force of 63 Stirlings, the attack was successful. The remaining 283 aircraft, thanks to accurate PFF marking, delivered the heaviest raid of the war so far on the port. The port was attacked again on the 28/29, led by seven *Oboe* Mosquitoes. Again, the PFF marking was accurate and the vast majority of the 323 aircraft involved dropped their bombs in the port area.

It is quite possible that this period of relative inactivity was Harris' method of preparing his forces for a lengthy period of operations. It was Bomber Command policy that no major operations were flown on three consecutive nights but, from 26/27 March, the rules were broken when the first of four attacks began. Duisburg was not a good start because despite being led by nine *Oboe*-equipped Mosquitoes, five were forced to return early with technical problems. A sixth, Mosquito IV DK318, flown by Flt Lt L. J. Ackland DFC, and his navigator, W/O1 F. S. Strouts DFC RCAF, was last heard from in the North Foreland area, becoming the first operational *Oboe* Mosquito loss. The remaining Mosquitoes were left to carry out a *Musical Wanganui* over the city but with so few markers, large gaps were left in the centre without any TIs at all. The result was widely spread bombing so very little damage was confirmed.

The St Nazaire raid made up the third consecutive PFF contributed raid and Berlin, on 29/30 March, became the fourth. Simultaneously, 149 Wellingtons were led by eight *Oboe* Mosquitoes to Bochum but badly-timed *Musical Wanganui* and gaps in the marking resulted in a disappointing raid. Only four buildings in Bochum were recorded as hit, all at the expense of twelve Wellingtons shot down, this equated to 8% of the force. The Berlin raid, made up of 329 aircraft, fared no better. Badly forecast winds combined with icing made the long trip to Berlin unnecessarily difficult. The PFF claimed good concentrated marking but it was positioned south of the city and, combined with the main force arriving late, most of the bombing landed in open country. Like Bochum, the losses were higher than average with 21 aircraft failing to return. An 83 Squadron Lancaster and its crew was the only loss for 8 Group.

The RAF Pathfinders

April 1943 – More squadrons, more airfields

The month began with the formation of a new unit which would hopefully eradicate any further inaccurate weather forecasts. No.1409 (Meteorological) Flight flew its first operational sortie, known as a PAMPA (Photographic Reconnaissance and Meteorological Photography Aircraft) on 2 April and was the only flight made by a Bomber Command aircraft that day. The 1409 Flight was one of two which were formed from 521 Squadron based at Bircham Newton. The new flight was officially formed at Oakington on 1 April as a lodger unit alongside 7 Squadron; the airfield at this stage was still under 3 Group control. The first sortie, a weather reconnaissance flight over Brittany in preparation for another U-boat pen raid, was flown by Flt Lt P. Cunliffe-Lister and his navigator Sgt J. Boyle; the first of 1,364 sorties.

Despite unfavourable weather conditions, accurately forecast thanks to 1409 Flight, the Essen raid of 3/4 April went ahead. The PFF covered the operation by preparing a *Parramatta* and *Wanganui* attack but, on arrival over the target, Essen was found to be clear of cloud. The PFF still carried out both marking methods, confusing the main force of 348 aircraft. The bombing was still accurate and widespread, and damage was caused in the centre and western half of the city. Many crews described Essen's defences as more hostile than usual but this could be due to the fact that no Wellingtons or Stirlings were involved in this raid. These lower flying bombers usually took most of the flak for the Lancasters (over 200 took part in this raid for the first time) and Halifaxes. As a result, twelve Halifaxes were shot down, two of them crashing in England and nine Lancasters also FTR (Failed to Return). It was 83 Squadron that took the brunt of 8 Group's losses; three more Lancasters were lost, along with 21 aircrew, and 156 Squadron lost Lancaster I W4894 with another seven crew.

The weather dictated success or failure over Kiel on 4/5 April when 577 bombers took part in the largest 'non-1000' raid of the war so far. Dense cloud and strong winds left the PFF no choice but to use the Wanganui sky-marking technique, but parachute flares and such conditions do not mix. TIs were also dropped but these could not be seen through the cloud and an effective decoy fire also added to the problem. Resorting to a DR bomb run, very few bombs were reported to have fallen in the town while defending flak managed to knock down several of the twelve aircraft lost, two of them from 156 Squadron.

It was a similar story over Duisburg on 8/9 April when 392 bombers were dispatched. Thick cloud once again disrupted any chance of the PFF marking the target accurately. Even with nine *Oboe* Mosquitoes at the helm, the bombing was scattered and only 40 buildings were reported as destroyed. Losses were high again as the nicknamed 'happy valley' defences poured deadly flak into the sky. Twenty aircraft were lost, including 7 Squadron Stirling I R9199 and 156 Squadron Lancaster I ED622 which crashed near Cologne. The following night, a smaller force of 104 Lancasters led by five Mosquitoes returned to Duisburg. Covered in thick cloud again, nearly all of the main force bombed on the Mosquitoes' sky-marking with only limited damaged being caused.

The situation did not improve during a raid on Frankfurt on 10/11 April. Solid cloud faced the PFF again and a large number of the main force claimed to have bombed on the glow of their TIs through the cloud. No one on this raid had any idea whether they were bombing on a TI, decoy fire or dummy fire and the raid was a failure. Twenty-one aircraft were lost, including three from 8 Group.

The training of Pathfinder crews and, in particular, the navigators was raised to a new level on 10 April, with the formation of the Pathfinder Force Navigation Training Unit (PFFNTU). Formed under the control of 8 Group, the PFFNTU was established at Gransden Lodge. As its title implies, the task of the unit was to train crews, selected from Main Force squadrons, for pathfinder duties. On 17 June 1943, the unit moved to Upwood, an air party being established at Warboys with effect from 11 June. Establishment at this time was four Stirlings, six Halifaxes and four Lancasters. With the Stirling being withdrawn from front-line operations later in the year, the establishment changed again to nine Lancasters and nine Halifaxes.

On 5 March 1944 the whole of the PFFNTU was moved to Warboys, by which time the Mosquito was introduced. Fourteen Mosquitoes were on establishment by December 1944, plus fourteen Lancasters and fifteen Oxfords. The PFFNTU was disbanded on 18 June 1945.

Harris was becoming restless with the lack of damage being caused in spite of large forces of bombers being dispatched. Bennett called for a change of tactic in an effort to tighten up attacks that were taking place within *Oboe* range. A modified version of the visual ground-marking technique *Newhaven* was developed where the PVM worked closely with the H2S-equipped aircraft. The H2S would drop blindly and then these were marked again with contrasting colours by the PVMs. It was over Stuttgart on 14/15 April that the PFF carried out its first official *Newhaven* attack with 462 aircraft taking part. The PFF claimed to have marked the centre of the city but, in fact, the first TIs landed on the north-north-east side and it was from here that the first bombing developed. With the target clear, the bombing started to 'creepback' in a north-easterly direction following the line of the attack. Attempts by the backers-up to re-mark the target either failed or marked further along, aggravating the creepback still further. Useful damage was still inflicted on the districts of the city, but the tendency for the bombing to creepback from the AP was never fully rectified by Bomber Command.

Another stepping stone was reached towards strengthening 8 Group on 15 April.

RAF Oakington, north-west of Cambridge, the home of 7 Squadron from 1940 to 1945 and under 8 Group control from 1943 onwards. At least 20 Lancasters can be seen at their dispersals resting from the previous night's operations. (via Author)

Oakington was finally placed under 8 Group control and 7 Squadron which had been serving there as a lodger unit since 1941 was now part of the station's strength. Two more airfields, Bourn and Gransden Lodge, were also placed under 8 Group in preparation for two more squadrons. The first, 97 Squadron, flying the Lancaster, was wrenched reluctantly from 5 Group, moving from Woodhall Spa to Bourn on 18 April. The second new 8 Group unit was selected from 6 (RCAF) Group. No. 405 (Vancouver) Squadron who were operating the Halifax moved from Leeming to Gransden Lodge on 19 April. Within days, both squadrons were in action. Bennett hoped that the increase in strength would give the group the ability to mark targets for longer and with a greater concentration.

Two raids that involved the PFF took place on the night of 16/17 April. A complicated plan to attack the Skoda armaments works in Pilsen was the largest raid of the night. Because this was a difficult target to attack, the PFF, leading the total force of 327 aircraft, were only operating as guides and the main force was briefed to identify the target themselves once the town had been illuminated. Once the PFF dropped their initial guiding TIs, the vast majority of the main force bombed onto them rather than carrying out the brief. Even with the PFF illumination and a moonlit night, many of the main force mistook a large asylum in Dobrany, seven miles to the south-west, as the Skoda factory. Only six crews brought back bombing photographs that were within three miles of the target. To add to the misery, 36 aircraft were lost along with 250 aircrew, five of them from 8 Group. In contrast, an excellent *Newhaven* attack was being carried out by 271 bombers over Mannheim. Accurate marking saw 130 buildings destroyed and at least 3,000 damaged. Forty-one industrial buildings had their production completely halted or seriously reduced. Wellingtons and Stirlings as usual took the brunt of the losses on this raid but 8 Group all returned home. The night for Bomber Command as a whole was a disaster, with a total of 54 aircraft lost, making this the worst night of the war so far. The only consolation was that fourteen aircraft came down in the sea homeward bound and several aircrew were rescued.

Far beyond the range of *Oboe*, Stettin and Rostock, 600 and 500 miles from England respectively, were chosen as targets on 20/21 April. A total

After being 'poached' from 5 Group in April 1943, 97 Squadron returned to Lincolnshire in April 1944 and remained there for the rest of the war. (via Author)

of 339 crews were briefed to fly as low and as long as possible over the sea, while eleven Mosquitoes of 2 Group made a diversionary attack on Berlin. Visibility was excellent as the force approached the target and the PFF began the third *Newhaven* of the month. Six PVM aircraft delivered their flares onto the A/P thanks to good illuminators. The backers-up maintained the marking throughout the raid which was delivered with equally devastating accuracy. Over 100 acres of the city centre were destroyed and thirteen industrial buildings, including the Pommersdorf-Milch chemical works, were totally wiped out. When a PRU flight was made the following day, 24 fires were still burning. The all-Stirling force taking part in the Rostock raid were nowhere near as successful. Their target was the Heinkel factory at Marienehe, north-west of the city centre, but on arrival, the target was completely obscured by a very effective smoke screen. The bombing was scattered and there were no reports that the factory was even hit let alone damaged. Twenty-one aircraft were lost on the Stettin raid, two of them from 8 Group. Eight Stirlings failed to return from Rostock, none of them from the PFF.

Having settled into their new homes, it was time for 97 and 405 Squadron to carry out their first operations with 8 Group. Their baptism of fire was a 561-strong raid to Duisburg which was occupying far too much of Bomber Command's resources. The PFF claimed to have marked the centre of Germany's largest inland port but a visit by the PRU the following day begged to differ. The PFF had in fact marked the north-eastern quarter of the city and the bombing by the main force appears to have fallen in this area and further afield. Some damage was caused, including 300 buildings destroyed, but it was not the attack that Harris or Bennett had hoped for. Two aircraft were lost from 8 Group out of the seventeen that failed to return. One of them was 405 Squadron Halifax II JB920, the first since joining 8 Group.

The last major raid of April 1943 was another trip to Essen on 30 April/1May. As cloud was expected, the PFF tactic was to sky-mark using just the *Oboe* Mosquitoes. Pessimistically written off as probably not working as well as ground-marking, the raid went remarkably well. Out of the force of 305 aircraft taking part, 238 claimed to have bombed Essen.

May 1943 – Mounting losses

Dortmund was selected for the first time as a target on 4/5 May. A force of 596 aircraft, the largest 'non-1000' force so far, initially used green TIs to mark the target so as not to confuse the reds being simultaneously used on a minor PFF H2S training operation to Rheine, 50 miles to the north. The marking was accurate in Dortmund but the backers-up, dropping red flares, slightly undershot and the bombing began to creep back. Half of the force managed to bomb within three miles of the AP, despite the best efforts of a decoy fire, which did attract nearly 300 bombs. Damage was extensive with 1,218 buildings destroyed and over 2,100 damaged, including the Hoesch and Dortmunder Union steel factories. A total of 693 people were killed and over 1,000 injured giving a grim but new record for a Bomber Command attack. It was also a bleak night for the crews who did not know that the weather had taken a turn for the worse over England. The raid may have been a success but by the time the last bomber had landed, 42 aircraft had either been shot down, abandoned or crash landed, the majority because of poor weather over their home airfields.

Harris was determined that the fourth raid on Duisburg on 12/13 May would make up for the lack of success from the previous attacks. One thousand, five-hundred sorties had already been flown by Bomber Command on Duisburg since October 1940. A total of 572 bombers were detailed for the raid, loaded with 1,559 tons, a record amount for a single target. The attack went like clockwork, the *Oboe* marking using red TIs was accurately backed-up by greens and the bombing was concentrated. Severe damage was caused throughout the centre and port areas by 85% of the crews who claimed to have bombed within three miles of the A/P. Over 1,500 buildings were destroyed and thousands more were damaged, including four August von Thyseen steel factories. In the port area, the bonus prize of sinking 21 barges and thirteen other ships, weighing in at 18,921 tons, was gratefully received by Harris. Another six ships of 41,000 tons were also damaged. Escalating fires tore through Duisburg and returning crews could still see them as they crossed the Dutch coast for home. Duisburg was not attacked again during the Battle of the Ruhr. No. 8 Group lost another four bombers, including two from 156 Squadron. One of them was flown by Sqn Ldr L. Verdon-Roe DFC, the son of Sir Alliott Verdon-Roe, the founder of the Avro aircraft company in 1910. The family had already lost a son serving with 102 Squadron in July 1941.

The increased effectiveness of the German night-fighter was in evidence when the majority of Bomber Command crews were stood down from operations for nine days during a full-moon period. Some operations did take place, the most significant being Operation *Chastise* by 617 Squadron on 16/17 May. Once again, 5 Group showed that they were the specialists when it came to precision bombing. The PFF were not inactive during the stand-down either, flying less glamorous and less dangerous *Bullseyes* which were simulated operational sorties for the benefit of OTU (Operational Training Unit) and HCU (Heavy Conversion Unit) courses.

Air Cdre Bennett and his staff also took the opportunity to move from Wyton into Castle Hill House, Huntingdon, on 15 May. With expanding staff since becoming a group, the Pathfinder Force HQ was controlled from this location until it disbanded on 15 December, 1945.

Operations began again on 23/24 May and Harris was determined to remind Germany that Bomber Command was still active. The largest non-1,000 bomber raid operation of the war so far, totalling 826 aircraft, was unleashed on Dortmund making it the biggest single attack of the Battle of the Ruhr. The PFF also achieved a record by managing to dispatch more than 100 aircraft for a single operation for the first time. In clear weather conditions, eight Mosquitoes accurately marked the centre of the city and the backers-up performed perfectly. The attack was carried out in two waves and the best 250 crews of all the groups involved were selected for the first one. They were instructed only to bomb on a TI and, if they did not see one, they should go round again until the next wave passed. The raid was a resounding success, with over 2,000 buildings destroyed, the concentrated bombing killing nearly 600 people and injuring 1,275. A large number of industrial buildings were also destroyed, including the Hoesch steelworks which ceased production. The attack was so successful that Bomber Command did not attack Dortmund for another year.

Essen, on 27/28 May, was saved by the weather despite a valiant attempt to sky-mark the target by the PFF. The force of 518 bombers caused only limited damage compared to previous attacks on this target with just 488 buildings

EF361 of 7 Squadron was one of two Stirlings that were brought down from the blast of a 77 Squadron Halifax, which exploded after being attacked by a night-fighter on the Dusseldorf raid on 25/26 May 1943. EF361 came down near Jülich, killing Plt Off J. F. E. G. Berthiaume and his six crew. (www.ww2images.com)

destroyed. The bombing was so scattered that at least ten other Ruhr towns were struck by bombs. Four 8 Group aircraft were lost this night; three of them fell to night-fighters, including 109 Squadron Mosquito IV DZ432 which crashed at Bleskensgraaf. Flt Sgt C. K. Chrysler RCAF managed to bail out but his navigator Sgt R. H. Logan RCAF was killed. DZ432 was the first *Oboe*-equipped Mosquito to fall on enemy-occupied territory.

The most successful raid of the Battle of the Ruhr came on 29/30 May. The target was the long, narrow town of Wuppertal, in particular, the Barmen part of the town to the north-east. The actual target was only two miles long and less than a mile wide but the accuracy with which the PFF marked this narrow strip of land was superb. The raid was almost a disaster when *Oboe* equipment failed, leaving an uncomfortable gap between the reds being dropped and the backers-up dropping their green TIs. The crews of 83 and 156 Squadron, all H2S-equipped, acting as the backers-up, kept the A/P marked with an accuracy that had never been seen before and has rarely been surpassed since. Credit must also go to the first wave of the 719-strong force who planted their IBs directly around the markers, giving all who followed behind a good target to aim at. Large fires quickly developed within the narrow streets of the town and what was experienced by the people of Wuppertal was probably the first example of a firestorm. Over 1,000 acres, approximately 80% of the built-up area in Barmen, would be destroyed by fire. Industry was almost wiped out with five out six of the town's big factories completely destroyed and an additional 71 damaged. Some 611 of the force came home with photographic proof that they had bombed the target but 33 more aircraft failed to return, the vast majority falling to night-fighters. It was the Me110s of NJG1 that claimed most if not all of the kills that night, pursuing many of the bombers out over the North Sea. All of 8 Group's losses were from 35 Squadron and all were shot by night-fighters, the only consolation being that, out of the four crews lost, fourteen survived to become POWs. Many combats took place and, in reply, at least seven Me110s were shot down.

June 1943 – More Mosquitoes!

On the last day of May 1943, 2 Group flew its last sorties before it left Bomber Command to join the new 2nd Tactical Air Force (TAF). The following day, two of its Mosquito units, 105 and 139 (Jamaica) Squadron, along with their current base, Marham, were transferred to 8 Group. To bring 105 Squadron up to speed with regard to *Oboe*, a section of 109 Squadron was transferred to it, giving 8 Group two Mosquito squadrons with the same capability. The introduction of 139 Squadron was an excellent piece of foresight from Bennett. Initially used as a 'supporting squadron', the unit was used for early marking and was particularly effective at carrying out diversions, drawing away many night-fighters from the main attacks. However, what Bennett had instigated within this squadron were the building blocks to a much larger all-Mosquito force which would come into its own from early 1944.

Following another full-moon stand-down, Harris called for a maximum effort attack on 11/12 June. No. 8 Group were involved in two attacks, the first by far the largest, was a second attempt to bomb Düsseldorf. A total of 783 aircraft, including 202 Halifaxes, the most ever dispatched of this type in a single raid, took part in the attack. The attack started well with the thirteen Mosquitoes involved dropping their red TIs accurately on *Oboe*. However, a combination of late backing-up and one Mosquito accidentally dropping a load of TIs 14 miles north-east of the city, meant that the raid was not the success it could have been. A large proportion of the main force bombed on the stray TIs and the enemy's decoys. But despite these distractions, a large amount of the bombing fell on Düsseldorf, destroying approximately 130 acres of the city and becoming the most effective attack on this target of the war. The partial success came at a cost for Bomber Command, losing 38 aircraft – only one of them from 8 Group.

The other attack taking place this night was an all-8 Group operation involving 29 Lancasters of 83 and 156 Squadrons, 22 Halifaxes of 35 Squadron, and 21 Stirlings from 7 Squadron. The target was Münster and the attack was a large-scale H2S trial to give new crews experience of using the equipment. The raid also had the dual task of experimenting with a new three-colour system to improve *Newhaven* attacks. Thirty-three of the force carried markers or flares, while those behind acted as the bombing force. After the first wave dropped their TIs, they all carried out a second run to bomb themselves. Accurate marking was reported and the raid was over in ten minutes, but post-attack photography showed significant damage to the city's railway installations and surrounding residential area.

Cologne had not been touched since the start of the Battle of the Ruhr, but on 16/17 June, the first of four attacks in the space of three weeks took place. One hundred and fifty Lancasters of 1 and 5 Groups were led into battle by 42 heavies from 8 Group. Sixteen of the PFF, equipped with H2S, were ordered to drop sky-markers on the target, which was cloud-covered. The attack did not go well, with several H2S sets going unserviceable combined with a late start to the marking. One hundred aircraft tried to bomb but this was scattered, while the remainder, because of the deteriorating weather, turned for home. On the surface, the raid would appear to have been a failure, although several significant buildings were hit. This was of no consolation to the fourteen Lancasters that were lost, including four from 8 Group.

Two operations were flown by the same PFF aircraft on the same night for the first

The RAF Pathfinders

time on 19/20 June. The first main target was the Schneider armaments factory at Le Creusot, involving 290 bombers from 3, 4, 6 and 8 Groups. The plan was for the PFF to drop flares over the factory and the main force were briefed to identify and attack the target rather than bombing on TIs. Two runs were to be made at approximately 5,000 ft, each dropping two small sticks of bombs because of the size of the target. By now though, the vast majority of crews were almost indoctrinated into bombing on TIs and many had great difficulty in making a visual identification of the factory. All bombed within three miles of the target, but being so small, only 21% of the bombs actually hit the Schneider works. A section of 52 PFF bombers, 26 of them H2S-equipped, then split off from the main force and headed 4 miles further south, to attack the electrical transformer at Montchanin. The H2S aircraft which dropped flares over Le Creusot, did the same again over the transformer and once again, the smaller main force were ordered to visually identify the target. Unfortunately, the majority mistook the target for the Henrie Paul iron and bronze works. Allegedly some of the crews did identify the correct target but still bombed on the lead aircraft's TIs.

No.5 Group made use of four 97 Squadron Lancasters on an interesting raid on the Zeppelin works at Freidrichshafen on 20/21 June. The raid was to be controlled by a single senior pilot and would go on to be known as the Master Bomber technique, which had its roots in the Dams raid back in May. No.5 Group, who were operating 56 Lancasters, provided the Master Bomber who, for this pioneering raid was Gp Capt L. C. Slee. However, en route, Slee's aircraft developed engine trouble and he had to hand over to the Deputy Master Bomber, Wg Cdr G. L. Gomm, OC 467 Squadron. Like Le Creusot, the raid was intended to be carried out at only 5,000 ft, but with the moon shining brightly and heavier flak defences than expected, Gomm ordered the force to climb higher to nearly 15,000 ft. Only one PFF Lancaster, flown by Flt Lt J. Sauvage managed to drop his TIs, but these were within 200 yards of the target. The attack was made in two parts: the first, all controlled by the Deputy Master Bomber, was to bomb Sauvage's TIs, while the second was a timed DR run from a point on the shore of the Bodensee. Approximately 10% of the bombs dropped hit the small factory and further damage was caused to various industrial sites, which was a good result considering the complexities of the operation. Two of the 97 Squadron Lancasters were badly mauled by flak while over the target, but the ace in the hole for the attack was that it continued onwards to North Africa, outwitting a large force of night-fighters which were ready for them on the return journey. Fifty-two of the force, including two 97 Squadron Lancasters made the return via an attack on La Spezia on 23/24 June, once again without loss.

It was a different story over Krefeld on 21/22 June, although on this occasion the force involved was considerably larger. Some 705 aircraft were detailed on what was to be an epic raid, including twelve Mosquitoes equipped with the new 'K' *Oboe*. Eight of the Mosquitoes carried the normal load of three red TIs and one LB (Long Burning) red TI. The remaining four were carrying three red TIs, a single red LBTI and a time-delayed single red TI. The latter was set to start burning five minutes after hitting the ground as a precaution should the special equipment fail, which was still a common problem. Another fail-safe, if the initial marking failed, was 31 H2S bombers who were ordered to drop yellow TIs; no chances were being taking by 8 Group, with so many aircraft involved. The 37 backers-up were then briefed to drop their green TIs on the reds or the yellows. The marking was near perfect by the *Oboe* Mosquitoes and this was accurately backed-up by all, but one of the PFF heavies. The raid was divided up into six waves, the raid lasting from approximately 0130hrs to 0239hrs. The bombing was as good as the marking and 619 aircraft bombed on the markers dropping 2,306 tons, three-quarters of them within three miles of the centre of Krefeld. A fire quickly raged across the centre of the city, completely gutting 47% of the built-up area. A total of 1,056 people were killed, 4,550 more were injured and 5,517 houses were destroyed, which resulted in 72,000 losing their homes. The firestorm that quickly developed eventually resulted in 9,000 of 11,000 acres of the city lying in ruins. It was a truly devastating raid.

The full moon period was not quite over when the raid was flown and 30 of the 44 bombers lost that night were brought down by night-fighters. It was a particularly rough night for 8 Group, with twelve bombers lost, all of them experienced H2S crews. These losses highlighted a problem for Bennett that never went away; send too few crews and risk a lack of marking or send too many, exposing more senior crews, as in this case, to an unnecessary level of danger. Six of those lost over Krefeld were part of the 'insurance' backers-up for the *Oboe* Mosquitoes and their loss was little more than a waste of aircrew and aircraft. The night was particularly bad for 35 Squadron who lost six aircraft with eighteen crew killed and sixteen becoming POWs. Krefeld was a highly successful attack for 8 Group but was also at the greatest expense to men and machines since the group's formation.

It was now the turn of the Elbefeld half of Wuppertal to be attacked after the Barmen half was successfully destroyed back in May. A total of 630 aircraft set out on 24/25 June but even with good accurate PFF marking, a classic creepback raid quickly developed. It is thought that this could be put down to the recent pressure being endured by the aircrews and high losses also being incurred. Despite the bombing stretching into the western parts of the Ruhr, it was later estimated that 94% of Elbefeld had been destroyed and local reports stated that more bombs had fallen than on the previous Barmen raid. However, Bomber Command's high losses

No.105 Squadron and its Mosquito IVs, with their Merlin engines warming through, on display for the press at Marham. (Aeroplane, via Author)

The RAF Pathfinders

Si placet necamus *(We destroy at will) was a very appropriate motto for the activities of 139 Squadron who served with 8 Group from June 1943 to the war's end and beyond.* (via Author)

continued to mount with another 34 aircraft lost, including seven from 8 Group. This was the first time that 7 Squadron flew the Lancaster in anger and it also lost its first machine on this raid. Lancaster III LM327, being flown by 'B' Flight Commander Wg Cdr R. G. Barrell DSO DFC & Bar was attacked by a night-fighter of II./NJG3 being flown by Oblt Raht. All attempted to abandon the crippled machine but unfortunately Barrell's parachute failed to open and he plunged to his death. Two others in this experienced crew, who were all about to finish their second tour of operations, were killed but three survived to become POWs and Plt Off H. J. Hudson DFM evaded capture. Barrell was the third flight commander that 7 Squadron had lost in a single week. The squadron's conversion to the Lancaster was very protracted and it would continue to fly the Stirling into mid-August 1943.

A second trip to Cologne during the Battle of the Ruhr was planned on 28/29 June, with 608 aircraft taking part. The raid was destined to encounter a procession of setbacks but still managed to deliver the heaviest raid of the war so far on the city. Firstly, conflicting weather reports meant that the PFF had to prepare a dual plan, one for a clear target and the second far less reliable sky-marking in the event of a cloud-covered raid. It was the latter conditions that were found by the lead PFF aircraft, twelve of which were *Oboe* Mosquitoes, although five had to turn back with technical problems before reaching Cologne. Of the remainder, only six were able to drop markers, beginning seven minutes late and only intermittently. It was a recipe for a disastrous raid but the main force still delivered a devastating attack which included the destruction of 43 industrial, six military and no less than 6,368 other buildings. Casualties included 4,377 killed, over 10,000 injured and at least 230,000 left homeless.

July 1943 – The Battle of the Ruhr ends and the Battle of Hamburg begins

Another 635 aircraft arrived over Cologne again on 3/4 July, this time targeting the more industrial area, east of the Rhine. The PFF ground-marking, carried out by 13 *Oboe* Mosquitoes was extremely accurate and the backing-up equalled it, allowing the main force to perform another heavy raid. Twenty factories and at least 2,200 houses were completely destroyed and 80 more industrial buildings were seriously damaged. The night also saw the first use of the *Wilde Sau* (Wild Boar) technique by a new German fighter unit called Jg300, based at Deelen in Holland. Using the Fw190 and Bf109 the technique involved attacking the bomber force over the target using any form of illumination available, such as searchlights, TIs or fires on the ground to expose the enemy aircraft. Jg300 worked closely with the local flak units who would be instructed not to fire above a certain height, so the *Wild Boar* aircraft could operate without being shot down by their own side. Of the 30 Bomber Command machines lost that night, twelve were claimed by Jg300, although these had to be shared with the local flak unit who also claimed twelve! At least four bombers claimed that they were shot at by other friendly aircraft but these attacks would have come from Jg300, without the crews realising.

There were only the north-western and south-western areas of Cologne left to bomb when a smaller force of 282 Lancasters and six Mosquitoes of 1, 5 and 8 Groups returned again on 8/9 July. The Mosquitoes, faced with thick cloud cover, carried out very accurate *Oboe* sky-marking which the main force was able to bomb. Another nineteen industrial targets and 2,381 houses were destroyed, killing over 500 civilians. Losses were lower with seven Lancasters lost, including another from 97 Squadron brought down by a 5./NJG1 night-fighter at Bassenge in Belgium.

Since joining 8 Group on 1 June, 105 Squadron had been training hard to bring its *Oboe* skills up to speed. It had already had a taste of operations but, over Gelsenkirchen on 9/10 July, it would provide *Oboe* sky-marking alongside 109 Squadron for the first time. The two 105 Squadron crews on this historic raid for the unit was 'A' Flight commander Sqn Ldr W. W. 'Bill' Blessing and his navigator Fg Off G. Muirhead in DK333 and Fg Off W. Humphrey with his navigator Flt Sgt E. Moore in DZ485, who joined eight Mosquitoes of 109 Squadron. It was not to be an auspicious beginning – the *Oboe* equipment failed to operate in five of the ten aircraft taking part and a sixth dropped its sky-markers in error ten miles north of Gelsenkirchen. Local reports thought that the raid was meant for the neighbouring towns of Bochum and Wattenscheid, with only a handful of bombs falling on Gelsenkirchen.

The final Ruhr raid took place on 13/14 July when 374 aircraft attacked Aachen. This was an interesting raid, once again affected by the weather. A strong tail wind had brought the first waves of the main force right up behind the PFF, resulting in them dropping their bombs within minutes of the TIs igniting. This meant that a large amount of bombs were dropped accurately in a very short space of time. The result was described locally as a 'Terrorangriff of the most severe scale' and, from above, Aachen seemed to burst instantly into flames.

The only operation flown on 14/15 July was the beginning of regular 'nuisance' raids, which would become the calling card of the all-Mosquito Light Night Striking Force (LNSF). While sketchy, the LNSF was not officially recognised until early 1944, but 139 (Jamaica) Squadron was definitely both its founding member and most successful unit. Used by Bennett as a multi-purpose squadron, either to drop *Window* (Hamburg onwards) in front of a main force or to bomb independently, the squadron set the tone for all future members of the LNSF. The squadron moved from Marham to Wyton on 4 July and its first operation from its new home took place on 14/15 July. Eight aircraft made the long trip to Berlin, evaded all defences and successfully bombed the German capital. Unfortunately, the squadron suffered its first loss but possibly not to enemy action when Mosquito IV DZ515, flown by Fg Off R. Clarke and his navigator, Flt Sgt E. J. Thorne, crashed into the North Sea on the homeward journey. It was destined to lose more aircraft than any other Mosquito squadron to serve in 8 Group.

No.35 Squadron appropriately led an all-Halifax force from 4 Group in an attack on the Peugeot factory in Montbéliard on 15/16 July. The factory was in the middle of the town of Sochaux, close to the Swiss border and it was vital that the marking was accurate, to avoid French civilian casualties. Despite a clear moonlit night and very weak defences, the TIs were dropped at just 6,000 ft, but landed 700 yards beyond the factory. Local reports claim that just 30 bombs fell on the factory and over 600 more came down in the town, killing 123 civilians and injuring 336. Only 5% of the factory was damaged and production continued as normal the following day. It was not 8 Group's finest hour.

Because of the increasing number of Mosquito squadrons joining 8 Group, it was decided that it needed its own training unit. On 1 July, 1655 MTU (Mosquito Training Unit) moved from Finmere and 2 Group control to Marham, which was one of the reasons for moving 139 Squadron to Wyton. Warboys was used as a satellite and it is possible that Downham Market was also briefly used for this purpose.

Since the end of May 1943, Harris had been circulating orders to his group commanders telling them to prepare for a series of heavy raids on Hamburg. This important city, with its port and high population, had already been attacked 98 times; none of the attacks were heavy or particularly successful. Having escaped the '1000-bomber' raids flown in 1942, it was now time for Hamburg to feel the full might of Bomber Command. The first raid of 791 aircraft was planned for the night of 24/25 July, with 8 Group once again taking the lead. Far beyond the range of *Oboe*, it was up to the H2S aircraft to mark the target which, being a port, was a good shape for the system. This raid would also be the debut for *Window*, a simple but effective method of creating a false reading on the enemy's ground *Würzburg* and airborne *Lichtenstein* airborne radar sets. *Window* was made from strips of coarse paper exactly 27 cms long and 2 cms wide, with a thin strip of aluminium foil stuck to one side. It had been available from April 1942, but the fears of senior Bomber Command staff that the Luftwaffe would copy it to use on raids against Britain, never materialised. It was a terrible decision not to introduce it into service earlier and it is estimated that 2,200 aircraft were lost during this period, many of them through German radar-assisted defences. During the six raids that made up the Battle of Hamburg it was also estimated that *Window* saved over 100 aircraft which could have been lost to radar defences.

The plan by the PFF for this major raid on Hamburg was for a *Newhaven* combining H2S marking and PVM. If the latter could not identify the aiming point, Blind Markers would be brought in to drop yellow TIs. The 'belt and braces' plan did not stop there. The backers-up were briefed to drop on the PVMs red TIs or failing this, the MPI of the H2S yellow TIs. Another new player used for the first time on this raid was the Re-centerers. These crews were ordered to keep the raid as concentrated as possible; a very dangerous undertaking, exposing the aircraft to several passes over the target. The raid started reasonably well, although the TIs were a little scattered, but mainly around the city centre. Despite 8 Group's efforts, a very fast 6-mile-long creepback began but being so large, nearly all of the bombing spread itself across the city. In just 50 minutes, 728 of the bombers had dropped 2,284 tons, causing severe damage across the centre and north-western districts of the city. Over 1,500 people were killed, making this the heaviest raid inflicted by Bomber Command so far outside of the range of *Oboe*. Mainly thanks to *Window*, losses were light, with twelve bombers lost and 8 Group were lucky to escape with just one 35 Squadron Halifax written off at Graveley without injury to the crew.

Hamburg was given a brief reprieve on 25/26 July when 705 aircraft set course for Essen. One 83 Squadron Lancaster 'Q' had the privilege of carrying the commander of the US 8th Air Force, Brig Gen F. Anderson, as an observer during this successful raid. The Krupps works in particular suffered its worst raid of the war, along with 51 other industrial buildings. The following morning, Doktor Gustav Krupps suffered a stroke, from which he never recovered, but this was a blessing in disguise because it saved him from being charged with war crimes during the post-war trials. Anderson described the raid as 'One of the most impressive sights I have ever seen' and as Q-Queenie landed safely back at Wyton, there were many sighs of relief. This did not stop Anderson flying as an observer on the following raid as well.

One of the worst raids of the war for the German population was unleashed on 27/28 July when 787 bombers returned to Hamburg. On arrival over the target the PFF discovered that several fires were still burning from the raid two nights earlier and this was where most of the Hamburg fire crews were still working. This was the first of many factors that would see Hamburg experience a 'firestorm' of such magnitude that it would result in two thirds of the city's surviving population fleeing. The PFF marking was all dropped 2 miles east of the planned aiming point, which was supposed to be the city centre. Despite this, the marking was concentrated and well backed-up and very little bombing crept back. A total of 729 aircraft managed to drop 2,326 tons of bombs, the vast majority of which fell within an area only 2 miles long and a mile wide. The weather conditions, which were incredibly mild, coupled with low humidity and a lack of recent rainfall, made the centre of Hamburg a tinderbox. Large fires took hold in the Hammerbrook, Hamm and Borgfeld districts and as they grew, all competed for oxygen, creating a firestorm of epic proportions. The local fire service could do little as they were trapped and those who tried to tackle the fires in the eastern half of the city, found the roads blocked by the bombing. From above, the crews watched as a cloud of smoke rose up to over 20,000 ft and one member of 83 Squadron described the scene: 'It was a most unholy sight lit up by raging fires'. The fire continued to burn intensely for three hours and approximately 40,000 people died in what was mainly a residential area, many by carbon monoxide poisoning when the air was sucked out of their basement shelters. Following this devastating attack, 1,200,000 people wisely left the city as they were not prepared to suffer any more from the raids which would inevitably keep coming.

The third major attack of the Battle of Hamburg took place on 29/30 July and was opened by three 8 Group Mosquitoes which dropped *Window* a few minutes before the main force of 774 aircraft arrived. The marking was all by H2S again, but fell 2 miles further east than planned, in an area just south of the devastation caused by the previous attack. On this occasion it was not a problem because a large

The Mosquito IV Srs 2 was capable of carrying four 500 lb bombs as displayed here by these 105 Squadron armourers. (Aeroplane via Author)

4-mile creepback spread itself across the city into the Wandsbeck, Barmbeck, Uhlenhorst and Winterhude districts which had not been hit before. A total of 707 of the main force dropped 2,318 tons of bombs which caused some fires, but not on the scale of the earlier raid. With the majority of the population now evacuated, civilian casualties were considerable lower, but improved *Wild Boar* techniques took their toll on Bomber Command and 28 failed to return, with 8 Group in particular suffering high losses. One 7 Squadron Lancaster was lost, two Halifaxes from 35 Squadron and two Lancasters each from 97 and 156 Squadrons. Out of the 49 aircrew reported missing, only three from 35 Squadron survived to become POWs.

There was a large overlap between the end of the Battle of the Ruhr and the beginning of the Battle of Hamburg. The 273-strong raid on Remscheid on 30/31 July was seen as the last official Ruhr attack. The raid was marked by *Oboe* which was, for the first time, continuously available throughout the raid. This reflected in the accuracy of the bombing of such a small force which managed to destroy 83% of the town with just 871 bombs.

August 1943 – Peenemünde and the long road to Berlin begins

Thanks to a very large thunderstorm over Germany, Hamburg escaped relatively unscathed on 2/3 August. Of the 740 aircraft that took part, several were lost through severe icing, turbulence and possibly lightning strikes, including one Halifax from 35 Squadron. On a more positive note, although it still involved the loss of an aircraft, it was the beginning of the end of a three-year relationship between 7 Squadron and the Stirling. Plt Off W. E. Stenhouse in Stirling I R9260, one of 105 of the type taking part in this raid, had to return early to Oakington, with a misfiring port outer engine. As the bomber touched down, the undercarriage collapsed and the aircraft was written off, becoming the last Stirling loss for 7 Squadron. Since introducing the bomber to RAF service in 1940, the squadron had lost 120 of them in a range of accidents and incidents.

With a full-moon period now approaching, a switch to Italian targets could not have been better timed. Italy was already under pressure to capitulate since President Roosevelt had offered them favourable terms while, in stark contrast, General Eisenhower threatened heavy bombing from the air, if they did not. It was up to Bomber Command to carry out Eisenhower's threat and the first of several raids, began on 7/8 August. A total of 197 aircraft from 1, 5 and 8 Groups were detailed to bomb Genoa, Milan and Turin. The latter attack was led by Gp Capt J. H. Searby of 83 Squadron acting as Master Bomber. All but two of the bombers taking part claimed to have bombed one of three cities, although the Turin operation was the least successful of the three.

A much larger force of 504 aircraft returned to Milan on 12/13 August and encouraged by good PFF marking, caused a great deal of damage throughout the city. Simultaneously, a 152-strong raid was taking place over Turin which at the time was described by the crews taking part as 'heavy and concentrated'. While post-attack reports from Turin only describe a handful of people being killed or injured, it was undoubtedly Milan's worst raid of the war. Of the 1,174 people who were killed in air raids in Italy during August 1943, the vast majority of them were killed in Milan this night.

Milan was hit again on 14/15 August, this time with a 140-strong all-Lancaster force from 1, 5 and 8 Groups causing further damage to the city. The following night another all-Lancaster force claimed very concentrated bombing on the city, although on this occasion, seven aircraft failed to return. The final raid of this latest, and what would become the last, Italian bombing campaign of the war, took place on Turin on 16/17 August. A total of 154 aircraft from 3 and 8 Groups claimed to have bombed the centre of the city and successes included hits on the Fiat works and the Royal Arsenal.

Intelligence received by the British in June 1943, under the auspices of Operation *Crossbow*, revealed that the Germans were advancing at an alarming rate in their efforts to produce rocket-powered unguided weapons. Maps, sketches and reports provided by a pair of Polish cleaners working at the German Research Establishment at Peenemünde showed drawings of a 'rocket assembly hall', an 'experimental pit' and at least one 'launching tower'. It was clear that the V-1 and V-2 projects were reaching a critical point and it was imperative that development of both weapons had to be destroyed, or at least disrupted.

It was also clear that only Bomber Command had the ability to attack such a small target and the first phase of *Crossbow*, Operation *Hydra*, was planned for the night of 17/18 August. The sensitivity of the target was exemplified by the fact that only the COs of the squadrons taking part knew the routes and basic details of the raid. Even the armourers were not given particulars of bomb loads until after 1300 hrs. The raid itself featured several 'firsts', including the first use of an MB (Master Bomber) for a full-scale Bomber Command raid. This task was given to Acting Gp Capt J. H. Searby, who was the station commander of Warboys at the time. He would be flying an 83 Squadron Lancaster from Wyton, a unit he also had been in command of since May 1943. Searby's role in controlling and guiding the raid would become a significant factor in its ultimate success.

A total of 596 aircraft were tasked with bombing Peenemünde, made up of 324 Lancasters, 218 Halifaxes and 54 Stirlings. The plan was to attack three separate

A/Ps in three waves; the points were the scientists' and workers' accommodation, the main rocket factory and the experimental station. Both Red Spot Fire TIs and 'shifters' were used for the first time by 8 Group on this raid. 'Shifters', as the name suggests, were employed to re-mark, or shift, the bombing to the original A/P, or to a new one.

The raid took place in moonlight conditions with perfect visibility and the first wave had little difficulty finding the target. The defending flak was light and no enemy night-fighters had been seen en route or near Peenemünde. This could be credited to a successful diversion by 139 Squadron who sent eight Mosquitoes to Berlin. This was where the enemy fighter controllers thought that the main raid was going to take place. It was thanks to this 'spoof' raid that the first two waves of the attack escaped unmolested by night-fighters, but it would be a different story for the third wave from 5 Group.

It was not the best of starts for the attack when the first TIs fell too far south onto a forced labour camp. This was quickly turned around through the combined efforts of Searby and the 'shifters' but not before the labour camp was obliterated, killing up to 600 foreign workers, the majority of whom were Polish. After this serious error, the raid developed into an accurate attack and, by the end of it, approximately 560 aircraft claimed to have bombed one of the three A/Ps with 1,800 tons of bombs, of which 85% were HE. While no crucial equipment was totally destroyed, several senior scientists were killed and sufficient damage was caused to stall the V-Weapon projects for almost two months. This may not sound very long, but it did also make German senior staff reconsider their plans to move the establishment into a more obscure inland location. This move was already in the planning stage before the attack but once this had happened, the process was accelerated. By October 1943, the entire production operation was moved to Mittelwork and this crucial delay may have saved the Allies and, in particular, Britain, from an even larger V-1 and later V-2 attack.

By the time the third wave of bombers were carrying out their run over Peenemünde, every available night-fighter from as far south as the Ruhr, was redirected towards the north German coast. The night was so clear the bomber crews could see the fighters closing in on them from all directions, apart from below. It was from this position that the Luftwaffe operated, for the first time, a pair of night-fighters fitted with *Schräge Musik*. This was a simple but effective system and was among others, fitted to the Bf110G-4 where a pair of 20mm MG FF/M machine guns were positioned in a near vertical position, behind the pilot. While the crews were fending off fighters from all directions, a pair of Bf110s slipped under the bomber stream and in short order shot down six bombers between them. A further 34 bombers failed to return, the vast majority from that final wave and virtually all

Group Captain J. Searby, who carried out the role of the Master Bomber, for the first time over Peenemünde on 17/18 August 1943. (via Author)

from 5 and 6 Group who lost twelve out of 57 aircraft taking part producing an alarmingly high casualty rate of 19.7%.

For 8 Group, the night was a total success from the start, with good marking and a well-orchestrated raid, thanks to Searby and the efforts of his crews. Losses were low for the group, with just two Halifaxes from 35 and 405 Squadron lost; the latter being the first aircraft brought down. As a footnote to the Peenemünde raid, despite the fact that the Germans had shot down 40 bombers, the chief of the Luftwaffe general staff, General H. Jeschonnek, was distraught about the attack. Not only had he ordered Berlin's defences to open fire on their own aircraft that night, he had totally miscalculated where the raid was going to take place. Already facing relentless pressure from Hitler and Göring about his ability to defend the Reich, Jeschonneck committed suicide on 18 August.

On 19/20 August, 139 Squadron made another long-distance foray to Berlin, losing another Mosquito from the small force of eight aircraft taking part. The I.G Farben factory in Leverkeusen was attacked again on 22/23 August without loss to 8 Group. The *Oboe* guided raid found thick cloud over the target and the vast majority of bombs fell wide of the target although partial success could be claimed, as most of them caused serious damage in Düsseldorf.

Arthur Harris now decided the time was right for another large raid on Berlin which had not been attacked en masse since March 1943. Much faith had been put in H2S and his senior staff were convinced that the crews who had been operating it during the previous months, had now gained enough experience to pinpoint and attack a major inland city. It was obvious that the pressure was building on 8 Group to help deliver a devastating blow on the German capital, which was probably the most unpopular of all targets throughout the entire war.

This would be another Master Bomber controlled raid, but this time the task would be undertaken by Wg Cdr J. E. 'Johnny' Farquier, the CO of 405 Squadron. Ottawa-born Farquier was a highly experienced pilot, having gained over 3,000 flying hours before the war began. During the Peenemünde raid he was Deputy Master Bomber and flew 17 times over the target, guiding the waves of bombers into the aiming points; a task he undertook so well he was awarded the DSO for his actions in September 1943. The raid would be the largest assault on Berlin so far, with 727 aircraft made up of Lancasters, Halifaxes, Stirlings and 17 Mosquitoes taking part. The latter were used for marking the route to target although this did not stop a large batch of aircraft deviating from the briefed course as they approached Berlin. Ahead of the main force, the PFF as usual led the way but, frustratingly, the H2S failed to identify the centre of Berlin and lead aircraft proceeded to mark an area on the southern outskirts of the city. Flak and defending fighters were prevalent and the first of many victims of the night belonged to 8 Group.

Lancaster III JA678 flown by OC 'B' Flight, Sqn Ldr C. J. Lofthouse OBE, DFC was shot down by night-fighters near Oranienburg, although all eight crew managed to jump to safety before becoming POWs. The eighth crew member was Gp Capt A. H. Willetts DSO, Oakington's Station Commander. Willetts was no stranger to flying with his crews which he did, not only from a morale perspective but also to gain experience himself of flying on a raid over Germany. This policy of senior RAF officers flying on operations was deeply frowned upon and this would be the last time a senior commander from Bomber Command would undertake such a mission.

By the time the last aircraft had bombed, approximately 575 claimed to have dropped on a TI despite the fact that the bulk of the attack had fallen outside of Berlin. It would have been impossible for those crews following behind to tell the difference between a TI or a fire on the ground as fires in the residential areas of Lankwitz and Lichterfeld took hold. Further damage was caused to industrial targets in Mariendorf, Marienflede and Templehof, all of which were located south of the planned attack on the city. Some bombs did, more by accident than design, fall in the city centre into the 'government quarter' where it was later recorded that not a single building in the Wilhelmstrasse was undamaged. Despite the fact the marking was inaccurate, Berlin recorded its worst raid of the war so far, with 2,611 individual buildings destroyed or damaged, as well as no less than twenty vessels sunk on the city's canals. Casualties were high as well, with 854 people killed, although the vast majority of these were caught out in the open before taking cover in their air raid shelters.

Continued faith in the power of H2S was shown again on 27/28 August when 674 aircraft, including an all 'Y' equipped PFF aircraft, set out for Nuremburg. En route, 47 PFF aircraft were ordered by the MB to check their equipment by dropping a single 1,000 lb bomb on Heilbronn. Only 28 managed to carry out this order which, according to later reports, fell in the northern part of the town and was presumed to be an attack on an industrial area of Heilbronn. On arrival over a cloud-free Nuremburg, the initial PFF marking was accurate, but a creepback developed very quickly which, despite the efforts of the MB (of whom only 23% of crews taking part claimed to hear his broadcasts) and the re-centerers, could not be halted. A large number of bombs fell outside the town and local reports stated only that the bombing was scattered across the south-eastern and eastern suburbs. Plt Off R. King and his 83 Squadron crew had great difficulty in placing their visual marker in the right place and were forced to descend to 14,000 ft to drop it. At this height they were now at the mercy of the flak and after dropping their TIs and HE were hit by light flak which damaged the hydraulics. On return to Wyton, only one wheel would come down but King managed to carry out a good crash landing without injury to the crew.

Up until now, both Monchengladbach and Rheydt had escaped a serious attack from Bomber Command but on 30/31 August this was about to change. A large force of 660 aircraft of all types was despatched for a 'double attack' on both towns led by the PFF. In good visibility, *Oboe*-equipped Mosquitoes of 109 Squadron led the way and accurately marked the centre of Monchengladbach for the first stage of the attack to begin. Twenty-two minutes into the attack, the Mosquitoes diverted their marking to the centre of Rheydt, where the remainder of the attack was carried out with exemplary accuracy. Later described as 'a model' of good PFF marking, extensive destruction and fire damage was caused to both towns. In Monchengladbach alone, over 1,000 buildings were destroyed, nearly 20% of them industrial, while in Rheydt, considerable damage and disruption were caused to the large marshalling yards there.

It was a busy night for the PFF's Mosquitoes who were also flying an operation to St Omer that night. The first of many small raids into northern France to bomb ammunition dumps had begun, all flown by OTU crews so as to give them the experience of bombing on PFF markers before they were posted to a front-line squadron. The target was a large bomb dump at Foret d'Éperlecques, north of St Omer and crews from 26, 29 and 33 OTUs, all flying Wellingtons, were taking part. They were led by six *Oboe* Mosquitoes and six Halifaxes of 8 Group and the attack was successful, with at least one large explosion witnessed by several crews. However, two crews from 26 and 29 OTU were lost, the latter having to ditch owing to an engine fire.

The month ended with another long haul to Berlin, with 622 aircraft taking part, plus a handful of Mosquitoes once again marking the route. On the night of 31/1 September, the Germans successfully employed the use of 'fighter flares' for the first time. The flares were not only dropped along the bomber route into the target but also on the way, giving the enemy night-fighters the opportunity to hunt at will within the bomber stream. Combined with the increasingly efficient searchlight co-operation which worked especially well over the target, it resulted in 47 bombers being shot down, including three from 8 Group. Many bombers were shot down before they reached the target and, combined with an inaccurate weather report, this raid was by far the worst since the introduction of the TI method. The marking was dropped south of the city centre but the psychological effect of the enemy fighters resulted in the vast majority of the main force bombing early and a creepback developed that was 30 miles long!

The PFF were very lucky this night to have got away with just three casualties; one of these being the loss of Lancaster III JA916 of 97 Squadron being flown by the unit's CO, Wg Cdr K. H. Burns DFC. When just minutes from the target, the Lancaster was attacked head on by an Fw190 which set the whole of the port

Late 1943 – 500 lb bombs being prepared for the Mosquitoes of 139 Squadron, at Wyton. (via Author)

wing on fire. Without hesitation, Burns ordered his crew to bail out although his bomb-aimer paused and asked if he could jettison the bombs. Burns quickly replied 'No, leave 'em be and I'll aim the kite where they'll do some good'. Once he was sure his crew had left, Burns trimmed the bomber nose down but just as he was leaving his seat, the bombs exploded, blowing the Lancaster to pieces. Incredibly, three and half hours later Burns woke to find himself lying under some pine trees. As the pain started to creep into his body, he discovered that his right hand and half of his forearm was missing but it felt normal without any pain coming from it. Despite discomfort from his right ankle and foot he stood up to find that his ripcord had not been pulled and barely enough of his parachute had opened to slow his descent. Realising he quickly needed help because of the large amount of blood he had lost, he staggered across a field and lay down near a signal box where he was eventually found. Doctors later discovered that one of his lungs had also collapsed and the other was saved by the ripcord being wrapped around his neck! He was treated well by the German doctors but when he was later moved to Dulag Luft he complained of back pain. It was discovered that this was broken as well and when the resident German doctor asked why this had not been picked up earlier, he was told that the X-ray department had been destroyed by the RAF! Wg Cdr Burns was later repatriated, fitted with a false arm and returned to flying duties.

September 1943 – Varying targets

Owing to the high loss rate of the Stirling and Halifax on recent trips to Berlin, the operation on 3/4 September was to be an all-Lancaster affair. No. 8 Group would also supply four Mosquitoes to drop 'spoof' route flares to put the enemy night-fighter off the scent. A force of 316 Lancasters were detailed for this attack, of which 81 were from 8 Group, made up of 55 Markers and 26 Supporters. Approaching the city from the north-east, bombing was concentrated on the industrial area of Charlottenburg, Wedding and Siemensstaddt which had not suffered a serious attack before. Many factories were hit and utilities, including a major water and electrical works, were put out of action. Some 422 people were killed and if Goebbels, Berlin's Gauleiter, had not ordered the evacuation of all children and adults not engaged in war work, the casualty list would have been higher. The loss of 22 Lancasters on this trip, which equated to an unsustainable 7%, technically meant that the raid was a failure. As predicted, 8 Group took another beating with 7 Squadron losing three Lancasters, plus one each from 97 and 156 Squadrons.

There were clear skies over Mannheim on the night of 5/6 September, giving

Pathfinders the opportunity to perform a copybook *Newhaven* raid. This would be a double attack which would involve Ludwigshafen as well. Route-marking flares guided a force of 605 bombers to a point 5 miles south of Luxembourg, from which a direct run to target was made. The Pathfinders took a slightly different route over Kaiserslautern, 34 miles west of Mannheim, making a timed run to the AP which was positioned on the eastern edge of the town centre. The marking was extremely accurate and the hand-picked crews at the front of this big raid dropped their bombs directly onto them, getting the 40-minute raid off to an excellent start. The inevitable creepback of bombing fell directly into the centre of Mannheim causing total devastation and what few post-attack records that were taken simply record 'a catastrophe'. Ludwigshafen suffered almost as badly, with the local fire departments having to deal with nearly 2,000 individual fires, with at least three of them described as 'fire areas'. For Bomber Command the raid was a total success, although another 34 bombers failed to return. No.8 Group lost a Lancaster from 83 and 156 Squadron and 405 Squadron lost its last Halifax in action before fully converting to the Lancaster.

Over the next few days, several heavy-bomber Pathfinder squadrons were stood down but the Mosquitoes were still hard at work. The bombers were back in action again on 15/16 September, leading a medium-sized raid against the Dunlop rubber factory at Montluçon, central France. All the major bomber groups contributed to this raid, with the exception of 5 Group, which was becoming an increasingly common thing as the Lincolnshire-based squadrons continued their own agenda. A total of 369 aircraft took part, including another five 8th Air Force B-17s, all under the control of MB, Wg Cdr D. F. E. C. Deane. The raid was an outstanding success and virtually every building in the factory was either destroyed or damaged.

It was to France again on 16/17 September for a similar raid to that staged on Montluçon, but this time without a Master Bomber. In fact, for some unknown reason, this effective technique was not re-established until the spring of 1944. The same four bomber groups contributed another 335 aircraft and again, five more B-17s joined for the experience. This time the target was the strategically important railway yards at Modane, not far from the Italian border. However, the success of Bomber Command's last big raid was not repeated and poor marking resulted in a weak attack.

There was no let up for the Mosquitoes, with further small attacks against Berlin, Cologne and Emden on the same night as a large raid on Hannover was launched. It had been two years since this city had been attacked but Bomber Command were taking no chances and two divisionary raids were also organised, both flown by 8 Group. Some 711 bombers took part in the main raid, again including five 8th

Fg Off V. Brammer (in cockpit) and his 7 Squadron crew at Oakington in the summer of 1944 after they had completed an operational tour with 8 Group. (Mike Garbett and Brian Goulding collection)

Air Force B-17s, who were on their first night raid into Germany. The marking was a little off-target, thanks to the winds being much stronger than forecast. The concentrated bombing fell within an area that was approximately two to five miles south-south-east of the city centre, although several fires in this area were started and several industrial buildings were damaged. As the main raid progressed, 21 Lancasters and eight Mosquitoes carried out an effective spoof on Oldenburg. Large bundles of *Window*, flares and TIs gave the impression that a much larger raid was about to unfold. Twelve more 8 Group Mosquitoes also attempted a similar spoof on Emden and it is believed that the combined efforts of the two diversionary attacks did reduce the loss rate, which still stood at 26 aircraft.

It was a return to Mannheim on 23/24 September, with the intention of destroying the northern part of the city which had escaped the previous raid. Good weather allowed the PFF to organise a *Newhaven* attack and those crews and the front of the raid, managed to drop their PVMs directly onto the aiming point. Of the 628 bombers taking part, almost 500 dropped their bombs on the aiming point, with only the rear wave creeping back, but still causing damage to the I.G. Farben factory in the northern suburbs of Ludwigshafen. The devastation in Mannheim was meticulously recorded and although only 102 people were killed, a further 25,000 were bombed out of their homes. Such was the success of this raid, Sir Arthur Harris decided that a third heavy attack against the city was unnecessary until further notice.

Once again 8 Group provided 21 Lancasters and eight Mosquitoes on a diversionary raid but, on this occasion it was not successful because the target, Darmstadt, was little more than 20 miles from Mannheim. Those few German night-fighters who were duped by the diversion could see where the main attack was occurring and quickly headed towards the main force. A large proportion of the 32 bombers lost this night were night-fighter victims, including one of the two Lancasters lost from 97 Squadron.

A total of 678 aircraft returned to Hannover to make amends for the attack five nights earlier. Once again the wind played its part and the attack developed five miles north of the city centre aiming point. However, at least 582 bombers performed the most concentrated piece of bombing during the whole of 1943. Over an area of just 15 square miles, a record-breaking 130 tons per square mile was dropped, flattening the Brink district of Hannover. While this was obviously not the objective, the main force had performed impeccably, while the spot light was once again on the PFF. The group was redeemed though by the blind bombing of the Supporters, who dropped their bombs directly onto the aiming point.

The now traditional diversionary raid was more successful than the last. Some 21 Lancasters and six Mosquitoes attacked Brunswick, causing considerable damage and managing to draw several night-fighters away from the main raid as well. In the case of Lancaster III LM345 of 405 Squadron, this tactic was a little too successful as it fell victim to a night-fighter. Sqn Ldr L. E. Logan DFC RCAF and his crew managed to bail out and survive to become POWs, except Flt Sgt G. L. Watts who managed to evade capture.

Nine other PFF Mosquitoes also did their bit to draw away a few night-fighters during a diversion to Emden but 38 bombers still failed to return from Hannover, four of them from 8 Group. No.35 Squadron lost a Halifax, while 7, 156 and 405 Squadrons lost a Lancaster apiece, the latter being the first loss since fully converting to the type.

The month ended on a high for 8 Group, with a *Musical Parramatta* to Bochum on 29/30 September. This *Oboe*-assisted raid involved 352 bombers and, after the lead Mosquitoes dropped their red TIs accurately into the centre of the town, these were bolstered by a concentrated group of green TIs by the backers-up. This superb piece of marking encouraged the main force to drop over 1,000 tons of HE into the middle of the town with devastating results. This was a total success for 8 Group which was marred by the loss of four of its aircraft. One of these was Mosquito IX LR506 of 105 Squadron which was the first example of this new mark flown by the unit. Virtually within sight of their home airfield at Marham, the Mosquito crashed near West Raynham, killing the navigator, Plt Off L. Hogan DFM.

October 1943 – High price for a new target

Before we look at the first raid of October 1943, the activities of the 83 Squadron armourers at Wyton are worth studying. It was not uncommon for the senior staff to change their mind about which target was going to be visited that night and 1 October was no exception. Each raid would not only dictate the amount of fuel taken, but also the bomb load would change from target to target, making the armourers' job one of the toughest on the station.

On this particular day, the aircrew had been on standby all morning when the call came through to prepare thirteen aircraft to Stuttgart. The usual long and complicated process of preparing for the night's raid began but, as the armourers prepared to bomb-up, the plan was changed to Hagen. At this point, the Flight Sergeant in charge of the operation disappeared to the Sergeants' Mess, where he could express his opinion out of earshot. Just as all the aircraft had been de-bombed, at 1500 hrs, Stuttgart was back on again! Unbelievably, after all the aircraft were bombed-up again, the target was switched back to Hagen and probably for the sake of the armourers alone, was finally kept that way. To quote 83 Squadron's

ORB, 'On regaining their sanity, the armourers de-bombed again and visited the chapel for prayers'!

The raid on Hagen went like clockwork for 8 Group which, on this occasion, also included 1 and 5 Groups. A total of 243 Lancasters and eight Mosquitoes found the target cloud-covered but, thanks to some exceptional *Oboe* sky-marking, the bombing was accurate. Unbeknown to the crews, at least 46 industrial companies were destroyed, including a factory which produced accumulator batteries for U-boats. As the Hagen raid was coming to an end, twelve more 8 Group Mosquitoes were attacking a steelworks at Witten on a training sortie. Eight Mosquitoes managed to bomb Witten while two others, whose equipment had failed, added to the devastation in Hagen.

On 2/3 October, 294 Lancasters of 1, 5 and 8 Groups, with a pair of 8th Air Force B-17s tagging along, attacked Munich. Despite taking part again in another large multiple group raid, the Lancasters of 5 Group almost operated independently which, on this occasion, did not work well. Despite visibility being very good, the first wave of PFF marking was not up to its usual standard. It was, however, placed generally in the centre of the city and the early waves of bombers caused a great deal of damage in the south and south-east of Munich. No.5 Group was bringing up the rear on this raid and employed its 'time-and-distance' bombing method, ignoring the PFF marking. A 15-mile creepback developed along the route into the city, with a huge waste of bombs falling harmlessly in open fields. A total of 339 buildings in Munich had been destroyed, with 191 people dead, but it could have been so much worse.

The first of two trips to Kassel during the month was planned for the night of 3/4 October. A force of 547 aircraft, of which 80 were Mosquitoes and Lancasters from 8 Group, set off towards a hazy target. The ground haze was so bad that the H2S blind-markers overshot the A/P and the visual markers could not get a good enough view of the target. These conditions were perfect for the Luftwaffe to drop a trail of decoy flares, which took nearly a third of the main force away from the intended target. Of the aircraft that did attempt to bomb near the A/P, many of them fell in the western suburbs, small towns and villages on the outskirts of Kassel. This was not all bad for the attacking bombers because at least seventeen major factories were seriously damaged – three of them were high-priority targets. The suburb of Wolfshangar also took a pounding and a large ammunition dump to the north at Irlingshausen was also hit. One of the largest of its kind in Germany, the site erupted in a violent explosion, drawing in more bombers. At least 84 buildings were destroyed in the military complex which was pockmarked with craters, one of them over 300 ft in diameter.

A separate diversionary raid was staged again by 8 Group, with ten Mosquitoes attacking Hannover. Twelve more took part in the first of many attacks on the Knapsack power station near Cologne and four flew a Mk.II *Oboe* trial to Aachen; all the Mosquitoes returned safely.

The next trip to Frankfurt on 4/5 October would be the last Bomber Command raid in which the USAAF would take part. It was also the first serious raid on Frankfurt of the war and a combination of clear weather and good marking dealt the city a bitter blow. The eastern half and the inland docks were particularly heavily hit and the post bombing report described both as a 'sea of flames'. The diversionary raid against Ludwigshafen was larger than normal at 66 bombers, mainly because of 1 Group's participation. While the marking and bombing were not up to usual standard, it looks like it did draw some attention from the main raid because just thirteen bombers were lost from the 406 taking part. Unfortunately for 8 Group, three of them were theirs. Two Lancasters, one each from 97 and 156 Squadrons were lost with their crews over Germany, while Halifax II HX148 of 35 Squadron crash-landed. The Halifax with Flt Lt D. R. Wood at the controls had been badly damaged by flak over the target after having been coned and hit repeatedly for nearly five minutes. One engine was knocked out as Wood set course for home and a second failed as he crossed the Dutch coast. The third engine failed over the channel and it was while attempting a single engine approach into Biggin Hill that the final motor gave up and the bomber crashed not far from the airfield's perimeter. Luckily all escaped, although four of the aircrew were injured.

Worthy of mention are the activities of a single 8 Group Mosquito on 4/6 October which was carrying out the first operational trail of the G-H blind bombing system. While it was unsuccessful on this occasion, this radio-navigation system would become another weapon in Bomber Command's armoury.

The Hannover raid on 8/9 October would be the last Bomber Command raid for the Wellington. The 26 'Wimpies' that took part in this raid were all very lucky to make it home unscathed, because the German night-fighter controllers guessed the target correctly very early on, despite the largest diversionary raid organised so far. A total of 504 bombers set course for Hannover and, before reaching the target, the enemy night-fighters were weaving in and out of the stream, despatching victim after victim. Despite this, the clear conditions produced good marking, with the TIs glowing brightly in the centre of the city for the first time. The creepback was contained to just two miles, resulting in the worst attack on Hannover of the war. Several key industrial targets, including the Continental rubber factory and the Hanomag machine works, had been severely damaged.

To counter Bomber Command success, the night-fighters had done their work well and 27 aircraft failed to return. No.8 Group had taken it on the chin, with five aircraft lost, made up of two 7 Squadron Lancasters, a 35 Squadron Halifax, plus a Lancaster apiece from 97 and 156 Squadrons. Once again the 35 Squadron's loss was an epic tale, where the crew were lucky to make it back to friendly soil. Badly shot up by a night-fighter not far from the East Anglian coast, Fg Off M. M. Muller and his crew in Halifax II HR777 desperately tried to reach the emergency landing field at Woodbridge. Missing it completely and momentarily lost after the attack, but convinced they were over England, the bomber crash landed. All seven crew escaped with injuries after their bomber caught fire at Bridge Farm, Bradfield, near North Walsham. Over Gemany it was a grimmer tail for the pilot of 97 Squadron Lancaster III JB174 after the bomber was hit by flak. Plt Off G. D. Nicholl RCAF was over the target when a violent explosion removed the nose of the Lancaster and a large section of the port wing. The main fuselage immediately caught fire and the bomber began to enter an unrecoverable spin. Nicholl was unable to communicate with his crew because the initial blast had ripped off his flying helmet and he must have hoped that they were all making their escape. Although Nicholl would not have known it at the time, the rest of his crew perished in the crippled Lancaster while he was lucky and survived to become a POW.

The destruction of Hannover continued again on 18/19 October, with an all-Lancaster force of 360 aircraft taking part. Unfortunately, the target was cloud covered and the PFF were unable to accurately mark the centre of the city. Most of the bombing fell in open countryside which was a disappointing end to the series of raids on this target.

Things did not improve a great deal with the next raid on a new target and it was a particularly rough night for 8 Group. Up until now, Leipzig had not been seriously attacked with a sizeable force of bombers, but on the night of 20/21 October, 358 Lancasters from 1, 5, 6 and 8 Groups attempted to make amends. This was one of the furthest targets taken on in force since the beginning of the war. It was a 1,100-mile round trip for the 8 Group aircraft and they were the closest of all the Bomber Command groups. The weather on this operation was described in records as 'appalling' which is just about all that was recorded about this unsuccessful raid. Bombing was simply described as scattered and of the 271 Lancasters that did manage to bomb, no reports of any serious damage were ever made. To add insult to injury, another sixteen Lancasters failed to return, unfortunately including six more from 8 Group, and of the 42 aircrew missing, only four survived to become POWs. The same night the PFF Mosquitoes were out in force, with 28 of them attacking Berlin, Cologne, Brauweiler and Emden. It did not all go their way either, with two from 139 Squadron failing to return back to Wyton.

With over a week of October 1943 left to run, Bomber Command flew its last major raid of the month with a large force being sent to Kassel. It would be the most devastating raid on this city and once again Bomber Command would pay a very high price for their success.

A total of 569 bombers made up of 322 Lancasters and 247 Halifaxes set course for Kassel unaware that the German night-fighter controllers had successfully predicted the target very early on. On arrival over Kassel, the PFF marking was carried out blind using H2S, but some sharp-eyed visual markers realised that they had overshot the target and the marking was skilfully moved to the centre of the city. Despite a batch of German decoy markers diverting a few bombers, the main force accurately bombed the city centre, resulting in one of the most devastating attacks on a German city since Hamburg's firestorm back in July. A smaller firestorm did begin in Kassel but not as powerful as in Hamburg. The damage was extensively recorded and the statistics are difficult to comprehend. Sixty-three per cent of the city's living accommodation was rendered unliveable, with 155 industrial buildings including three Henschel aircraft factories seriously damaged and 78 public buildings, 38 schools, 25 churches and 16 military and police buildings destroyed. Bodies were still being recovered at the end of November, by which time the toll had reached 5,599; a third of these were unidentifiable.

November 1943 – Battle of Berlin begins

It had been ten days since Bomber Command had been out in force and, to make amends, a large raid was organised against Düsseldorf, with a larger than usual diversion against Cologne. Düsseldorf was by far the larger attack with 589 aircraft taking part, including 38 Lancaster IIs from 3 and 6 Groups, all equipped with H2S. This would be the first time H2S was used on a large scale but unfortunately the equipment was still not up to the task.

The bulk of this raid fell on the centre of Düsseldorf, but deteriorating record-keeping by the Germans does not allow a clear picture to be built of how successful this raid was. The Cologne diversion with 52 Lancasters and ten Mosquitoes, all from 8 Group, was excellent in all respects. Reports from Cologne describe the raid as accurate, with almost all the bombs falling in the city centre. Only seven people on the ground were killed, which gives an idea of how deserted Germany's big cities were becoming. All aircraft involved returned safely.

It was an all-Mosquito night again on 5/6 November, with 26 taking part in small attacks on Bochum, Dortmund, Dusseldorf, Hamburg, Hannover and Leverkusen. The latter would claim another 105 Squadron Mosquito and an experienced crew. Flt Lt J. Gordon DFC and his navigator Fg Off R. G. Hayes DFC were only 30 miles from touching down at Marham, when they inexplicably crashed into a field at Road Green Farm, Hempnall.

Formed at Oakington on 12 November 1943, 627 Squadron was one of three squadrons transferred to 5 Group in April 1944. The squadron saw out its days at Woodhall Spa. (via Author)

Seven *Oboe* Mosquitoes attacked Cologne and Duisburg on 8/9 November and, the following night, another eighteen headed for the Ruhr. The target was the blast furnaces at Bochum and a steelworks at Duisburg. All escaped unscathed except Mosquito IV DZ492 of 109 Squadron which was hit by flak near the target. The crew, Plt Off R. E. Leigh and Plt Off J. Henderson, were unaware of how much damage had been caused until they crash-landed at Wyton. Just as the Mosquito touched down, the entire rear fuselage, tail and all, gracefully detached itself from the rest of the aircraft, without injury to either crew.

On 10/11 November, 313 Lancasters from 5 and 8 Groups set course for the Modane railway yards again. The PFF marking was very challenging once more, with the target being located in a valley with sides rising to over 11,000 ft. As in the previous attack, the marking seemed to overshoot and concentrated on the railway station. However, a creepback managed to cause serious damage to railway yards and 200 aircraft returned with target photos showing that their bombs had landed within one mile of the target. One interesting phenomena which was reported by the crews was a bizarre echoing and re-echoing off the mountain sides of their own bombs exploding.

A French target was tackled on 11/12 November when 124 Halifaxes and ten Lancasters attacked the marshalling yards in Cannes. Of this force, eighteen Halifaxes and the ten Lancasters were provided by 8 Group which, on approaching the target, set to work preparing a *Newhaven* attack from 5,000 ft. The TIs were concentrated but the yards managed to escape the worst of the bombing while the repair shops were damaged by blast. Many French people were out on the streets watching the spectacle, which took a turn for the worse when several bombs fell in the suburb of La Bocca and a village by the name of d'Agay. The German propaganda machine seized the opportunity to describe the RAF flyers as 'pure savages' in a local newspaper. The raid was a total success although four Halifaxes failed to return, three of them from 35 Squadron. Two were brought down on the homeward leg back over France by night-fighters. The third Halifax, HR929, being flown by Fg Off J. R. Petrie-Andrews DFC, DFM, had an engine failure en route, but still continued to the target and bombed successfully. Rather than turning back, Petrie-Andrews opted to continue on across the Mediterranean rather than risk being shot down by a night-fighter over France and, at best, a long stretch in a POW camp. As the fuel ran out, a perfect ditching was carried out off the Sardinian coast and, after the seven aircrew had spent a few hours in their dinghy, they were rescued by an Allied ship.

No. 8 Group gained another unit on 12 November, when 627 Squadron was formed at Oakington. The core of the unit was formed from 'C' Flight of 139 Squadron, so it was days before it became operational with its Mosquito IVs. This latest addition to the 8 Group armoury was another crucial jigsaw piece that would bolster the harrying and diversionary antics of the Mosquitoes. While not officially stated as such, the LNSF had been born.

The Mosquitoes were at it again on 13/14 November, with nine bombing Berlin and eight, using *Oboe*, hitting the blast furnaces at Bochum, again all without loss. Ten more Mosquitoes attacked Dusseldorf and three bombed Bonn on 15/16 November, but on this occasion one aircraft was lost from both raids.

The Mosquitoes continued this spell of attacks on 16/17 November, with another 21 attacking Cologne, Gelsenkirchen and Krefeld, while the rest of Bomber Command enjoyed a few days stand down. However, Bennett did not pass the full privilege to 8 Group, stating in signal to all PFF squadrons that they could be required at a moment's notice.

While the rest of Bomber Command enjoyed a few days' rest, 8 Group were called upon, at Bennett's suggestion, to carry out an H2S blind-bombing raid using TIs against Ludwigshafen on 17/18 November. The scientists who had designed H2S had been complaining that their equipment was not being used to its full potential and 8 Group would be perfect to test the boffins' theories. A separate batch of operations by 21 Mosquitoes was already planned for the same night on Berlin, Bochum, Duisburg and Bonn. The latter target would have a dual role as a diversionary raid for the 66 Lancasters and 17 Halifaxes that would attack

Ludwigshafen. On approaching the target, the German defenders fruitlessly started lighting decoy TIs and laying a smoke screen, both of which would be ineffective when H2S was employed. While not fully confirmed, the attack was a success with several fires started within the target area and at least two large explosions seen. Thanks to the four Mosquitoes and their little diversion, the night-fighters were drawn away from the main force and, as the heavy bombers approached their target, they saw the contrails of the enemy rushing to protect Bonn.

Bomber Command and Arthur Harris, in particular, were now ready to take on their biggest challenge of the war so far. Harris was convinced that an all-out attack on Berlin would bring Germany to its knees. In a letter written to Churchill on 3 November, Harris wrote, 'We can wreck Berlin from end to end if the USAAF will come in on it. It will cost between 400–500 aircraft. It will cost Germany the war.' Harris based his theory on the devastation that had been caused on Hamburg by 7,000 tons of bombs after just four attacks. Sixteen were planned against Berlin, but they would be spread over four months while the mayhem caused in Hamburg was compressed into just ten days. Berlin, though, was a much larger city and, despite the colossal tonnage that would be dropped on it, the damage caused by previous attacks would almost act as fire break. As the campaign developed, the effectiveness of Bomber Command continued to decline, as the night-fighters and increasingly efficient ground defences, took their toll. Half of Harris's prophecy in the Churchill letter would come true – the alarmingly high price that Bomber Command would pay.

The Battle of Berlin began on the night of 18/19 November, with 440 Lancasters and four Mosquitoes taking part. At the same time, the biggest diversionary raid of the war so far was also taking place, with 395 aircraft attacking Mannheim and Ludwigshafen; this raid would prove a little too successful for many of the crews.

The Berlin force found the city covered in cloud and the PFF had no choice but to mark and bomb blindly. The attack was also hindered by only eleven aircraft having a serviceable H2S and the marking that did take place quickly faded under the thick cloud; even skymarking did not work. However, the backers-up kept marking the target as best they could and at least 1,000 tons of bombs were dropped across the city. Large fires were started and four industrial targets were destroyed. Very few night-fighters were encountered as they appear to have been sent to deal with the Mannheim raid. As a result, only nine Lancasters were lost, including two from 8 Group.

Meanwhile, the Mannheim force also found its target covered in cloud and, despite a valiant attempt to mark the target, the bombing was scattered. Several industrial targets were still hit, including the Daimler-Benz car factory, whose production output dropped by 90% for 'an unknown period'. The night-fighters were in abundance on this raid and several scored multiple kills, mainly against Halifaxes and Stirlings. Some 23 bombers were lost, a dozen of them Halifaxes, including a 35 Squadron machine, nine Stirlings and a pair of Lancasters, including 7 Squadron's Lancaster III JA970. The latter was an experienced crew flying the last operation of their tour. None of the 8 Group's crews survived.

At the start of this raid there was much excitement at Gransden Lodge which had drawn in the Canadian press because of a single 405 Squadron machine. All eyes were on Lancaster X KB700 named the 'Ruhr Express', which was the first Canadian-built Lancaster to enter front-line squadron service. It would be an inauspicious first operation for KB700, which returned early with a technical problem. The 'Ruhr Express' only flew one more operation with 405 Squadron before it was transferred to another Canadian unit, 419 Squadron at Middle St George. The bomber was written off after its 49th operation; all the more frustrating because it was being planned for the Lancaster to return to Canada after its 50th!

The next raid on Berlin would set records and see the end of an era as Bomber Command's Stirlings flew their last operations over Germany. A total of 764 aircraft, the largest force despatched on a raid to the German capital so far, headed east, in appalling weather, on 22/23 November. The weather was poor en route but this did not bother the crews as the vast majority of enemy night-fighters were kept on the ground because of it.

It was the most successful raid on Berlin of the war but, with regard to losses, it was one of the worst for 8 Group who lost seven of the 26 aircraft that failed to return. Two were from 7 Squadron, one from 83 Squadron and two each from 97 and 156 Squadrons. Forty-five aircrew were lost and only four from 97 Squadron, Lancaster III JB238, survived to become POWs. Compare these figures to those killed on the ground which were at least 2,000 people, including 500 in a shelter at Wilmersdorf.

A smaller force of 383 aircraft headed for Berlin again the following night, strangely flying the exact same route as they had the previous evening. It would be a night of 'spoofing' and decoying, in an attempt to deceive the German controllers, despite the fact that they had identified the intended target very early. Fake communications by German-speaking controllers in England, both male and female achieved some more confusion. Eight Mosquitoes took part in this trip as well and several of them dropped 'spoof' fighter flares north of the bomber stream which also drew a few enemy fighters away.

The target was once again cloud-covered, so *Wanganui* was employed, combined with a good concentration of TIs. The PFF's efforts this night were almost irrelevant, because the bulk of the 303 aircraft that bombed could not

The first of many Canadian-built Lancasters was KB700, the 'Ruhr Express', which began operations with 405 Squadron on 18/19 November 1943. (via Author)

avoid the temptation of the eleven big fires that were still burning from the night before. A large amount of additional destruction was caused, although the exact details were hard to record by those on the ground, who were still coming to terms with the effects of the previous attack. One of several high-priority targets hit was the Rheinmental Borsig works which built tanks, torpedoes, bombs, shells and fuses. At least 45% of the factory was destroyed.

The loss statistics for 8 Group this night were even worse than the previous raid. Of the 20 Lancasters lost, nine of them were Pathfinders. No.7 Squadron suffered the most, with two bombers and their crews lost near the target but Fg Off P. K. B. Williams and his crew in Lancaster III JA971 did manage to make it almost back to Oakington. Hit by flak over the target, which was described as light by many crews because so many night-fighters were operating over the city, both elevators were shot away. On approaching Oakington, Williams ordered five of his crew to bail out, rather than risk trying to land the bomber with such crucial control surfaces missing. With just the pilot and navigator onboard, the bomber turned north and was totally abandoned to its fate and crashed at Welney Wash. All of the crew landed safely none the worse for the experience. No.83 Squadron had a bad day as well, losing its commanding officer Wg Cdr R. Hilton DSO, DFC and Bar, along with his crew in Lancaster III JB284. The bomber was hit by flak and crashed in the target area.

On 26/27 November, 443 Lancasters and seven Mosquitoes were mustered for another attack on Berlin. A more substantial diversion of 157 Halifaxes and 21 Lancasters also attacked Stuttgart, but both forces appeared as one until the formation reached Frankfurt. This manoeuvre proved quite effective, as the German controllers thought that Frankfurt was the main target, right up to the last moment.

Unusually, the weather over Berlin was clear and, after a long approach from the south, the PFF marked an area six to seven miles north-west of the city centre. The majority of the force did bomb that area but for even those who did not, their bombs still fell within the sprawl of Berlin. A total of 38 war production-related factories

were destroyed and the now wholesale destruction of housing and public buildings continued. One of the latter that was hit was the Berlin zoo which had already been bombed on 22/23 November. Very few animals were housed here now since, like the human population, they had been evacuated to other zoos in Germany but many of those that remained were killed in this attack At least one example of leopard, panther, jaguar and various apes had made their escape, though, only to be hunted and shot in the streets.

December 1943 – Nightmare over Berlin

The first of six major bombing raids that would take place during this month because of poor weather, was organised for the night of 2/3 December. A total of 650 aircraft was due to take off but because of poor flying conditions, the total was brought down to 458 aircraft, which included eighteen Mosquitoes and fifteen Halifaxes, the remainder were all Lancasters.

Setting course directly to Berlin, this should have been a straightforward raid but, unfortunately, the weather forecast issued to the crews was far from accurate. High winds kept pushing the bombers to the south and by the time the stream made it to Berlin, the majority bombed up to 15 miles from the A/P. Some damage was caused across Berlin but this would be a successful night for the enemy, in particular the night-fighter crews. Not only did Berlin's increasingly effective decoy system draw many bombers off, but the German controller also picked up very early where they were going. Night-fighters were waiting over Berlin in abundance and by the end of this poor operation, 40 aircraft, an alarming 8.7% of the force, had been shot down, including seven from 8 Group.

The weather continued to hinder progress during the month, but many crews would have been relieved to have a break. They probably did not expect it to last an unprecedented two weeks though. In the meantime, the Mosquito operations continued with increasing strength, with attacks on Duisburg and Leverkusen, 25 of them taking part in the latter. One of the biggest Mosquito raids so far, took place on 12/13 December when twenty headed for Essen, nine went to Dusseldorf and a single machine to Osnabrück. Bomber Command and, in particular 8 Group, were finding the Mosquito to be the perfect weapon for keeping up the pressure on the enemy without the risk factor involved in sending larger and more vulnerable bombers to targets deep into Germany. While the Mosquito attacks would continue to increase, they would never replace the big raids.

It was back to the grindstone for Bomber Command when Berlin was again the target on 16/17 December. A force of 483 Lancasters and ten Mosquitoes took a direct route to Berlin over Holland and northern Germany. From the Dutch coast onwards, the bombers had to contend with night-fighters all the way to the target, then even more were waiting for them near Berlin. Before the force had reached Hannover, at least ten bombers had already been shot down. However, the bombers fought back this night and five night-fighters were claimed as shot down, including one by Flt Lt L. C. Kingsbury RNZAF, who was only on his second PFF operation with 7 Squadron. The Lancaster was intercepted by an Fw190 north of Brunswick which attacked from the starboard quarter and opened fire at 350 yards. Kingsbury instantly reacted and pushed the bomber into a diving turn causing the cannon fire to pass harmlessly above the Lancaster. Now exposed to Kingsbury's air gunners, Fg Off E. G. Bedwell and Sgt E. Parr reacted as quickly as their skipper and opened fire on the enemy fighter sending it earthwards in flames and out of control. The fighter disappeared through 10/10ths cloud which was no thinner when the force arrived over Berlin. The PFF dropped a good concentration of *Wanganui* flares and the majority of the bombing fell within the limits of the city, causing a great deal of damage. The sustained bombing of Germany's capital had now rendered over a quarter of its living accommodation uninhabitable.

The same night, the first of a long list of attacks on flying-bomb sites in northern France began: 26 Stirlings and nine Lancasters from 617 Squadron were led by a dozen *Oboe*-equipped Mosquitoes from 8 Group. The operation involved two separate raids on targets near Abbeville, with the Stirlings attacking Tilley-le-Haut and the Lancasters, a site in a wood at Flixecourt. Neither was successful. The Mosquitoes were unable to get any closer than 450 yards for the Stirling raid and no closer than 350 yards for the Lancasters. The latter, carrying 12,000 lb bombs, dropped them to within 100 yards of the markers, but this was of no significance for a target as small as a V-1 launching site.

The PFF led a total force of 650 Lancasters, Halifaxes and Mosquitoes to Frankfurt on 20/21 December, having been briefed that the target would be free of cloud. The raid did not go well from the start, having been picked up by the German controllers after leaving the English coast. The force was accurately plotted all the way to the target and a large number of individual combats took place. One of these involved a 7 Squadron Lancaster III being flown by Fg Off D. W. Field which came under a sustained attack by a night-fighter over Holland. The hydraulic system was damaged, neither bomb door would open and both turrets were unserviceable, forcing Field to turn back for Oakington. Before the English coast was regained, the bomber was attacked again, which knocked out the port inner engine. Now without flaps and with a jammed undercarriage, Field did not relish the idea of making a belly-landing back at base with a full bomb load. While over Suffolk, Field gave the order to bail out and the bomber crashed two miles north-west of Halesworth.

Meanwhile, as the main force approached the target, the PFF found the target to be covered by up to 8/10ths cloud and the planned *Newhaven* ground-marking was abandoned. While the main force waited for the alternative, the Germans on the ground were quick to respond, lighting the Hensenstamm decoy fire site five miles south-east of the city. The enemy's decoy proved to be effective but the bomber force was so big and by now so strung out that the resulting creepback still fell across the city, causing a large amount of damage which changed a potentially disastrous raid into a reasonably successful one.

The night-fighters did not relent as the force turned for home and another Pathfinder crew were lucky to make it home. Plt Off G. P. R. Bond in his 156

Squadron Lancaster was intercepted three times during the flight back to Warboys. The first attack took place just as they left the target but the rear gunner, Flt Sgt R. Underwood gave the attacking Fw190 a three-second burst and no more was seen of him. The second attack came not long after and it was the turn of Plt Off C. H. Moon in his mid-upper turret to try and deter the attacking Ju88. The crew of the twin-engine fighter were made of sterner stuff and returned with accurate fire, wounding Moon in the lung and shoulder, as well as putting a hole in the port outer fuel tank, before breaking away below the Lancaster. Less than a minute later, the Ju88 returned, sensing that this bomber was for the taking but, at a range of 400 yards, Underwood opened up with another three-second burst, striking the enemy fighter, forcing it to break off its attack. Not giving up, the Ju88 pilot attacked for a third time, opening fire from extreme range and the continuous stream of fire eventually struck the Lancaster's starboard outer engine, setting it on fire. The starboard tyre was also punctured and further rounds buckled the wheel before Underwood managed to hit the Ju88 again, just as Bond dived the Lancaster to port. By now, two of Underwood's four .303in Brownings had jammed and the Ju88 crew must have been aware that defensive fire had stopped coming from the mid-upper turret. The final attack came from the stern but as the Ju88's fire passed below the bomber, Bond pulled the aircraft up in a corkscrew and immediately responded to Underwood's call to dive to starboard. At the same time Underwood gave the Ju88 another burst and this was finally enough to convince the German fighter to give up the fight. Ten minutes later, another night-fighter tried its luck but, by now, Underwood had cleared his guns and gave the enemy a determined response from all four Brownings. The enemy disappeared without firing a shot. Nursing the damaged bomber home, Bond carried out a near perfect landing at Warboys despite the damaged undercarriage. Plt Off Moon survived and eventually fully recovered from his wounds.

It was an eventful night for Sqn Ldr J. Sale and his crew in their 35 Squadron Halifax III HX328. Sale was tasked with being one of the PVMs that night and, after making five attempts to find the AP, flying lower and lower each time, eventually dropped his bombs at just 5,000 ft above the target. Retaining the TIs, Sale set course for Graveley and was one of the lucky few who was not harassed by an enemy night-fighter. However, as the bomber circled the airfield to land, one of the TIs exploded setting the rear turret and a wing on fire, filling the Halifax with smoke. Turning away from the airfield, Sale opened the throttles and climbed to 2,000 ft at which point he ordered his crew to bail out. Sale then trimmed the bomber and prepared to leave when he turned around to be faced with a very embarrassed Flt Lt R. L. Lamb, the mid-upper gunner, holding his burned parachute. Without hesitation or any thought for his own safety, Sale jumped back into his pilot's seat and turned back towards Graveley as fast as the burning bomber would travel. The bomber touched down, by now pouring flame and, with great skill, Sale steered the Halifax as far away as possible from any buildings. Lamb and Sale were out of the bomber before it stopped rolling and, after running at least 200 yards in full flying kit, threw themselves flat on their faces as HX328 ripped itself apart behind them. It was one of those classic moments as both stood up, brushed themselves down and calmly and, more importantly without injury, headed for the Officers' Mess.

No. 8 Group and the vast majority of Bomber Command made the most of a few days off over the festive season. It was, as expected, the Mosquitoes that started the proceedings off again, when ten attacked Duisburg, nine Düsseldorf and one to Cologne on 28/29 December without loss.

Lessons learned resulted in a more complex route to Berlin on 29/30 December when 712 bombers flew a long approach from the south, below the Ruhr, and then within 20 miles of Leipzig, turned north for Berlin. To add to the German controllers' headache this night, eight Mosquitoes carried out a spoof raid on Magdeburg, six more to Dusseldorf, five to Leipzig and three to Leverkusen. Night-fighters were sent to all of the Mosquito spoof locations and by the time the main force was over Berlin, very few were to be seen. Once again poor weather en route to the target also kept many night-fighters on the ground. An excellent display of sky-marking was carried out by the Pathfinders, with most of the bombing falling in the south and south-eastern districts of the city. Those crews arriving late over the target described a smoke plume that rose to over 16,000 ft and fires could still be seen glowing from 200 miles away. Only two bombers out of the 20 aircraft lost were from 8 Group.

The year ended with another attempt on a flying-bomb site which had been missed earlier in the month. Six PFF Mosquitoes led ten 617 Squadron Lancasters on 30/31 December but, once again, the markers were 200 yards off target and the 'Dambusters' dropped their bombs directly onto them. Yet again the target was untouched.

Operations

1944

January 1944 – Berlin takes its toll

The New Year began with another new squadron being formed, specifically for the use of 8 Group. No.692 Squadron, under the command of Wg Cdr W. G. Lockhart DSO, DFC, was formed at Graveley where it would remain until well past the end of hostilities in Europe. Equipped with the Mosquito IV, it would help to bolster the expanding LNSF.

The first operation of 1944 was another trip to the target that made aircrew groan in the briefing room. It was Berlin again, this time an all-Lancaster operation involving 421 aircraft. Despite a Mosquito diversion raid to Hamburg, Witten and Duisburg, the German controllers were not deceived and several bombers were shot down en route, especially between the two route-markers. Once again, the target was cloud-covered and the Pathfinders' sky-marking quickly went off the boil, resulting in very scattered bombing. It was also a very grim night for 8 Group because out of the 28 bombers lost this night, ten of them were PFF aircraft. What was equally alarming was the aircrew loss rate which left 61 dead and only ten surviving to become POWs.

The following night, a further raid on Berlin was as ineffective as the previous one, with another 383 aircraft having to endure night-fighters all the way to the target. The German controllers correctly guessed Berlin as the target some 40 minutes before the force arrived over the capital. More night-fighters congregated over Berlin which was where the bulk of the 27 Lancasters were lost this night. No.8 Group took it on the chin again, with ten bombers lost and 66 aircrew dead, just five living to see a POW camp. No.156 Squadron, who dispatched fourteen aircraft this night lost five of them, with only four airmen surviving from Sgt A. D. Barnes's Lancaster III JB317, which came down near Bremen.

The fledgling LNSF was at it again on 7/8 January over Krefeld, Duisburg and Hamborn. The only casualty of the night was Mosquito IV DZ435 of 109 Squadron which crashed near Swaffham, injuring both crew. The following night a force of 23 Mosquitoes set out to cause as much disruption as possible, while the heavies had a few nights off. Ten of them headed for Frankfurt, eight to Solingen, three to Aachen and a pair to Dortmund. It did not go all their own way, especially for 627 Squadron, who lost three aircrew and two aircraft as part of the Frankfurt operation. Mosquito IV DZ293 was being flown by the OC 'B' Flight, Sqn Ldr E. I. J. Bell DFC, with his navigator Fg Off J. R. B. Battle. It is not clear what happened to the duo but both ended their war as POWs. The second aircraft from the squadron lost this night was W4072 flown by Fg Off I. H. Hanlon DFC RNZAF and Fg Off F. K. Evans DFM. The twin-engined bomber crashed after losing power from the starboard engine and dived into the sea off East Mersea. Evans was killed but, thanks to some local help, Hanlon survived and returned to the squadron the following day. W4072 was the prototype IV and first flew on 8 September 1941.

The city of Brunswick, up until now, had not received a great deal of attention from Bomber Command but, on 14/15 January, the heavies were back out in force to change that. Some 496 Lancasters and a pair of Halifaxes were picked up very early by the German controllers who were not put off by eleven Mosquitoes flying to Magdeburg and six more to Berlin on a spoof. A large formation of night-fighters was gathering and eventually unleashed a concentrated attack as the bombers passed Bremen. The enemy scored success after success, both en route to Brunswick and all the way back up to the Dutch coast. A total of 38 Lancasters were lost, including eleven from 8 Group and once again 156 Squadron got the worst of it, with five bombers lost.

The losses this night could have been a lot worse, with a whole host of combats reported by the 8 Group crews alone. Sqn Ldr W. Riches, in his 97 Squadron Lancaster, was intercepted by an Me110 which opened fire from dead astern. As the night-fighter closed to 600 yards, the rear gunner, Flt Lt W. M. Booth, ordered his skipper to corkscrew to port as he opened fire at the Me110. The enemy aircraft continued to close and at 400 yards both rear and mid-upper gunners fired long bursts at the Me110 which struck its nose and fuselage. The pilot of the Me110 then seemed to throttle back as if to attempt to follow the bomber's corkscrew and looked as if he was going to ram the Lancaster. Booth ordered a dive to port and, at just 100 yards from the Lancaster, both gunners poured continuous fire into the Me110 until it burst into flames and dived away into the clouds. Both gunners felt certain that they could claim a kill. This was not the last encounter of the night for Riches' crew, whose gunners could do nothing against a long-range rocket attack by an Me210. The rocket exploded just ten yards from the rear of the Lancaster but it was enough to put both turrets out of action and damage both fins and rudders. The Me210, which was still out of range, followed up with cannon and machine-gun fire, striking starboard outer, starboard inner propeller, flap and puncturing the starboard tyre. Not giving up, the Me210 struck again, this time hitting the port inner propeller, elevator and hydraulics. Rounds raked the fuselage and main plane and Riches was wounded in the leg after several machine gun bullets entered the cockpit. Booth, who remained in his turret, had the last laugh by returning fire with a single gun while operating the turret by hand. The Me210 was hit several times and broke off its attack, probably confident that this Lancaster was not going to make it home. He was wrong, Riches, though wounded and with his aircraft in a very sorry state, made it safely back to Bourn.

Berlin on 20/21 January, involving 769 aircraft, was a disaster from a bombing point of view, despite the PFF sky-marking going according to plan. Because of the relentlessness of the raids on Berlin, reports on this particular raid were not received until another four raids had taken place on the capital. As a result, the raid was declared virtually ineffective which was no consolation to the crews of the 35 aircraft lost this night; five of them from 8 Group.

Magdeburg on 21/22 January was another unsuccessful raid which went wrong from the start, following the premature arrival of some of the main force ahead of the PFF because of a strong tail wind. At least 27 crews decided to bomb before the PFF began dropping markers, making the task of the PVMs nearly impossible because they could not identify the aiming point. The Germans were very sharp and, realising that no TIs had actually been dropped, began an elaborate simulation of a *Newhaven* attack with reds following greens, several miles away from the city. The TIs that were actually dropped on the aiming point were not as bright as the decoy and approximately 40% of the 648 crews taking part dropped their bombs on the decoy and returned home with bombing photos showing open fields.

The PFF were understandably furious about the indiscipline that had occurred and the opportunity for a good attack was wasted. On top of that, 57 bombers were shot down on the raid, three quarters of them to night-fighters. The Halifax, of which 224 took part, suffered the most, with an alarming loss rate of 15.6% which included four from 35 Squadron. No.8 Group also lost six Lancasters from 7, 83, 97, 156 and 405 Squadrons.

Berlin was attacked on 27/28, 28/29 and 30/31 January, with a total of 1,741 bombers, not including the usual feints and spoofs, in an attempt to keep the night-fighters away from the main force. On these three raids, which were all marginally successful, 112 bombers were lost (15 from 8 Group), the vast majority of them to night-fighters.

One of the diversionary operations involving 8 Group took place on 28/29 January, when 63 Stirlings, led by four PFF Halifaxes, carried out mine-laying in Kiel

Bay. The task was carried out five hours before the main Berlin attack and was the first time that the PFF supported a mine-laying operation.

February 1944 – Battle of Berlin comes to an end

The first two weeks of February 1944 were dominated by nightly Mosquito operations to several targets, including Berlin, Aachen, Krefeld, Duisburg and many more. The 'heavy' squadrons were all excused from operations for an enforced 16-day period because of a full moon and poor weather.

This period was broken up by a visit to several 8 Group stations by the King and Queen on 8 February, including Gransden Lodge, Graveley and Warboys.

Worthy of mention was the operation flown by 617 Squadron that evening on the Gnome & Rhône engine factory in Limoges. Led by Wg Cdr L. Cheshire, the twelve Lancasters could only bomb the small target by adopting a new method of marking at very low level. Cheshire overflew the lightly-defended factory three times to warn the French workers to evacuate, before dropping a load of 30 lb IBs from between 50 and 100 ft. The eleven Lancasters following behind, dropped a single 12,000 lb bomb apiece, ten of which scored a direct hit on the factory. No.5 Group went on to specialise in this form of low-level marking while 8 Group refused to entertain the method, despite operating a large number of Mosquitoes which would have been suited to the task.

The PFF heavies were back in action again on 15/16 February; 121 one of them leading 770 bombers to Berlin. This was the largest amount of aircraft sent to

Mosquito IV DZ637 began its service with 627 Squadron in late 1943. After a short spell with 692 Squadron the bomber returned to Oakington and 8 Group, only to be lost on an operation to Siegen on 2 February 1945. (via Author)

AOC 8 Group, accompanies King George VI and Queen Elizabeth during their brief tour of Pathfinder airfields in February 1944. (via Author)

Berlin in a single visit so far, with a bomb load of 2,642 tons between them. On reaching Berlin, after swinging north over Denmark en route to outwit the night-fighters, the large force found the German capital covered in 10/10ths cloud. This called for a *Wanganui* attack and flares were dropped at two-minute intervals throughout the 20-minute raid. Some 85% of the main force claimed to have bombed the target and Mosquitoes flying over the city a few hours later reported large areas on fire and smoke rising to over 20,000 ft. As usual, this did not come without a cost for Bomber Command and 43 aircraft were lost, including eight from 8 Group. Although Berlin would be attacked one more time, this raid marked the end of the 'Battle of Berlin', much to the relief to all who had survived them so far.

The PFF was also busy flying a host of diversions, all of which did not manage to draw a single night-fighter away from the Berlin raid. Twenty-three *Oboe*-equipped

Mosquitoes attacked five Luftwaffe night-fighter airfields in Holland, while four more PFF Halifaxes led another all-Stirling mine-laying operation in Kiel Bay. The main diversion was carried out by 23 PFF Lancasters on Frankfurt-on-Oder, where 147 buildings were damaged, 25 people were killed and 34 injured. All aircraft from these operations returned safely.

Mine-laying operations to Kiel Bay were now a regular diversionary event but, on 19/20 February, the German controllers only sent a handful of night-fighters to investigate while the remainder were held back for the predicted target of Leipzig. The force of 823 bombers, made up of 561 Lancasters, 255 Halifaxes and seven Mosquitoes were intercepted by night-fighters as soon as they crossed the Dutch coast and were harried all the way to the target. To make matters worse, a strong tail wind that had not been forecast saw many of the main force arrive too early, forcing them to orbit the target before the PFF began marking. Unfortunately, this caused the loss of four aircraft in mid-air collisions and another twenty to flak. An additional complication was that the target was cloud-covered but good sky-marking apparently resulted in a concentrated raid.

By the end of the operation, 44 Lancasters and 34 Halifaxes had been lost, the latter equating to 14.9% of those taking part. As a result, the Halifax II and V were withdrawn from operations forthwith, destined never to overfly Germany in anger again. However, the last sorties flown by the Halifax II were carried out over Stuttgart the following night, one more aircraft being lost in the process.

Scattered bombing over Stuttgart was carried out on 20/21 February by 598 aircraft while minor operations on 23/24 February saw another PFF first. Seventeen PFF Mosquitoes were despatched to bomb Düsseldorf, including a 692 Squadron Mosquito being flown by Sqn Ldr S. D. Watts. His Mosquito was carrying a single 4,000 lb 'Cookie', the first of 10,000 such bombs which were destined to be dropped on the Third Reich as far afield as Berlin by the LNSF.

The evening's activities, on 24/25 February, began in a novel way and continued to surprise the German controllers throughout, resulting in no night-fighters being present over the intended target at Schweinfurt. Firstly, 179 aircraft from OTUs flew a large *Bullseye* over the North Sea (a similar operation had been staged for the Stuttgart raid as well) followed by 24 Mosquitoes attacking enemy airfields in Holland. As the main force of 734 bombers took off, another diversion was carried out over Munich by seven Mosquitoes which, combined with the previous feints, managed to lift most of the defending night-fighters off the ground two hours before the main force arrived. On top of the diversions, the main force was split into two waves: the first with 392 bombers, followed two hours later, by a second, with 342 aircraft. The attack itself was spoilt by many bombers undershooting the target which was blamed, in part, on the backers-up. By the time the second wave arrived over the target, the enemy night-fighters were on the scene but, out of the 33 lost that night, only four were brought down by the Luftwaffe.

The final 'first' for February 1944 was also a model Bomber Command raid. On 25/26 February, the target was Augsburg, with 594 bombers taking part, divided into two waves. A series of diversionary raids were carried out north of the intended route which following a regular plan, was used by OTUs on leaflet raids, therefore not perceived by German controllers as being a 'live' raid. The controllers held most of their night-fighters back in the Holland area while 131 aircraft dropped mines in Kiel Bay again; 22 Mosquitoes attacked Dutch airfields and fifteen more attacked four towns north of the Augsburg route.

In crystal clear conditions, the first wave approached the lightly defended city and, following very accurate marking and equally efficient backing-up, 2,000 tons of bombs were dropped by the time the second wave was turning for home. The old town was completely obliterated to such an extent that the German media publicized the raid as the utmost example of 'terror bombing'.

March 1944 – Tactical targets increase

From 1 March to 16 March, five operations were flown in daylight for the first time by aircraft from 8 Group. A pair of *Oboe* Mosquitoes flew as 'formation leaders' on

Mosquito IV DZ344 after a wheels-up landing at Oakington in March 1944. The Mosquito was repaired and later served with 2 Group CS, 21 Squadron and finally 140 Wing, before being SOC on 12 June 1945. (via Author)

five days during the period, for a formation of 2nd TAF bombers. The targets were flying bomb sites and as soon as the formation saw the Mosquitoes' bombs fall away, they bombed at the same time. No losses were suffered by the Mosquitoes during these operations.

The month began for the 8 Group heavies with a trip to Stuttgart which was carried out successfully, despite the target being covered in dense cloud. The same cloud also helped to prevent the night-fighters from entering the bomber stream and only four bombers, one of them from 156 Squadron, were shot down as a result.

Some 117 Halifaxes of 4 and 6 Groups were led by six *Oboe* Mosquitoes on an attack against the SNCA aircraft factory, outside Paris, on 2/3 March. A similar operation involving the two groups was successfully led by the PFF on railway targets in the Trappes area as well on 6/7 March. Le Mans railway yards were singled out on 7/8 March and again on 13/14 March by Halifaxes of 4 and 6 Groups, once again led by the PFF Mosquitoes. Both were described as good attacks, the latter in particular credited with destroyed 15 locomotives and over 800 wagons. On both operations, the damage caused was described as enormous and no aircraft were lost.

March 1944 was another period of re-organisation and an increase in strength for 8 Group. Part of the expansion involved the group gaining the full use of Downham Market, Little Staughton and Upwood while Marham was reduced to care and maintenance to build three new concrete runways. The first move was 156 Squadron, making the short hop to Upwood from Warboys on 5 March, followed by the formation of 635 Squadron at Downham Market, operating the Lancaster, on 20 March. Three days later, 105 Squadron moved their Mosquitoes to Bourn, while Little Staughton prepared itself for the introduction of two more squadrons in April.

on 15/16 March, 863 aircraft returned to Stuttgart. Although they delayed the arrival of the defending night-fighters by flying as far south as the Swiss border, 37 bombers would be lost once the night-fighters caught up with the attack. Strong winds caused the lead bombers to be three to fifteen minutes late arriving but even so, the 2,735 tons of bombs dropped caused at least two large fires in the city.

Two heavy raids on Frankfurt, within four days of each other, caused untold damage on the city. Between the two attacks, which involved 1,662 bombers, 6,240 tons of bombs were dropped in what was described by the *Bomber Command Quarterly Review* as 'one of the most successful attacks ever made'. Very effective diversions, mainly due to 8 Group and its Mosquitoes harrying airfields again, saw low losses in the first attack of just 22 aircraft, while 33 were lost in the second, unfortunately six of them from the latter were from 8 Group. PFF marking in both raids was accurate.

The RAF Pathfinders

Although the 'Battle of Berlin' was effectively over, Harris decided to launch one last major raid of the war against the German capital on 24/25 March. A total of 811 aircraft, made up of 577 Lancasters, 216 Halifaxes and 18 Mosquitoes were all in for a rough night. Dubbed the 'night of the strong winds' just about summed up what occurred as the bomber stream was pushed south by a strong, not forecasted, northerly, scattering the bombers. On reaching the target, the PFF managed to achieve a reasonable concentration of red and green TIs but the *Wanganui* sky-marking that followed, when up to 9/10th cloud drifted in, was blown miles off target. A great deal of unintentional damage was caused but the night belonged to the flak crews who brought down seventeen bombers before they reached Berlin. On the return journey, a large percentage of the bombers were blown over the Ruhr and 50 of the 72 bombers shot down were claimed by flak, the rest falling to night-fighters. The 8.9% loss rate was grim and 8 Group lost seven Lancasters, including the first from 635 Squadron.

March finished with the incomprehensible 795-strong raid on Nuremburg which was flown in a full moon stand-down period. Not only that, the route was almost direct to the target and skirted two well-known fighter beacons en route. Don Bennett, who generally had some input into the route chosen to the target, later claimed that he was overruled following criticism of such a direct tactic. Only 34 Mosquitoes were employed on diversionary attacks on Aachen, Cologne and Kassel and, as a result, the scene was set for the highest losses for Bomber Command in a single raid of the war.

En route to the target, despite some cloud forecast, the night sky was clear and the bombers' condensation trails could be seen for miles. At least 82 bombers were shot down en route or over the target, the majority to night-fighters. On arrival over the target, the PFF dropped TIs, TI floaters and *Wanganui* flares east of the centre of the city. The bombing was a disaster and the crew reports were pessimistic; no PRU cover was flown over Nuremburg to check for damage. By the time this debacle was over, 95 bombers had failed to return, including a dozen Lancasters from 8 Group.

Little Staughton, the home of 109 Squadron's Mosquitoes from April 1944 to April 1945 and 582 Squadron's Lancasters from April 1944 to September 1945. (via Author)

Mosquitoes of 627 Squadron at Oakington in March 1944, only weeks before they were transferred to 5 Group at Woodhall Spa. (via Author)

April 1944 – 8 Group lose, 5 Group gain!

No. 8 Group gained another unit on 1 April when 582 Squadron was formed at Little Staughton from the 'C' Flights of 7 and 156 Squadrons. The latest Lancaster unit was joined by 109 Squadron from Marham the following day; both were destined to see out their days at Little Staughton.

Having already experienced attacking comparatively soft targets over France the previous month, the build-up to Operation *Overlord* began to gain momentum during April 1944. However, hitting Berlin was easy compared to the much smaller targets in northern France that the PFF were now being asked to mark and a new higher standard of bomb-aiming had to be achieved.

Another new Mosquito unit was formed at Downham Market in the shape of 571 Squadron on 5 April, 1944. Equipped with the Mosquito XVI during its brief existence, the squadron was moved to Oakington after a detachment at Graveley on 24 April. The squadron remained at Oakington until 20 July, 1945 when it was moved to Warboys, but disbanded on 20 September, 1945.

From 14 April, Bomber Command was under the 'direction' of General Eisenhower, the Supreme Commander of Allied Forces. This meant that Eisenhower could call upon Harris to divert his forces as and when needed, in support of *Overlord*, but he was still free to carry on with the area bombing policy. Harris had received notification of Eisenhower's plan several weeks prior to 14 April, hence the attacks on the French rail network, which was perceived as the main method of supporting the German army in the event of an invasion. Known as the 'Transportation Plan',

'Praecolamus designantes' (We fly before marking) was an appropriate motto for a Pathfinder Lancaster squadron. No. 582 Squadron was both formed and disbanded at Little Staughton between April 1944 and September 1945. (via author)

Bomber Command would go on to be allocated 37 of the 80 key targets and, long before *Overlord* began, the targets were all destroyed.

No. 8 Group saw more changes of its own during April, beginning with 627 Squadron being detached to 5 Group on 15 April, following a move to Woodhall Spa. Three days later, both 83 and 97 Squadrons were returned to 5 Group control

Wg Cdr A. G. S. Cousens of 635 Squadron who, while acting as Master Bomber for a raid on Laon railway yards, was shot down in Lancaster III ND508. (via Author)

and both units moved to Coningsby. All three squadrons were only supposed to be 'detached' from 8 Group, but none would return. The reallocation of these squadrons was supposed to be in accordance with a fresh policy of giving each group more individuality but, despite this, the PFF still led from the front for command operations. The loss of two 'heavy' squadrons could not have come at a worse time for Bennett. Reduced to three-quarter strength, the number of sorties

Unknown pilot and Wg Cdr W. J. R. Shepherd, OBE (right), 8 Group's Chief Intelligence Officer astride a 4,000 lb 'Cookie' at Graveley, taken in April 1944; Mosquito DZ692 is behind. (www.ww2images.com)

and, more importantly, the number of targets in need of marking, rose dramatically because of *Overlord*. From 1 April through to 30 September 1944, 8 Group flew 13,966 sorties which was only a few hundred less than the amount they had flown since its formation in August 1942.

Typical pre-invasion attacks took place on 18/19 April, with the PFF taking part in eight separate operations in the same night. Rouen railway yards, Juvisy junction, Noisy-le-Sec marshalling yards and Tergnier railway lines and yards were all bombed by a total of 827 aircraft, with only eleven bombers lost from these four raids. All four operations were controlled by an MB with varying degrees of success and accuracy needed to improve in order to reduce the amount of French civilian casualties. A separate operation by 28 Mosquitoes saw visits to Berlin, Osnabrück and Le Mans.

It was a mixed night on 20/21 April for 357 Lancasters and 22 Mosquitoes from 1, 3, 6 and 8 Groups who attacked Cologne. It was also the first major opportunity for 5 Group to show off its new low-level marking techniques over railway lines at La Chappelle, north of Paris. The Cologne attack was accurate and successful but was outshone by 5 Group which employed 617 Squadron to carry out low-level marking with several 8 Group Mosquitoes also taking part. Attacks on railway yards at Lens and Ottignes were also accurately carried out and only ten Lancasters were lost from these four raids.

The use of 'Controlled *Oboe*' had been implemented over French marshalling yards earlier in the month and on 30 April/1 May it was used again at Somain and Achères. Controlled *Oboe* was when Mosquitoes dropped different-coloured TIs before the main force arrived at zero-hour. The MB would then give directions to the main force, guiding them to the most accurately dropped TIs. Both the Master and Deputy also carried flares and TIs, while backers-up could also be called into play, all at the MB's discretion.

May 1944 – D-Day build-up

From 1 to 21 May, a small group of *Oboe* Mosquitoes flew as 'formation leaders' for the 2nd TAF. The objectives were small targets in northern France and 8 Group contributed aircraft on six daylight operations during the period, without loss.

Once again, it was rail targets that occupied most of the Group's time at the beginning of May, although the Luftwaffe airfield at Montdidier was selected on 3/4 May. A total of 84 Lancasters and 8 Mosquitoes, all from 8 Group, took part in the attack which saw four out of eight Mosquitoes drop preliminary markers for the heavy bombers. At least one batch of green TIs landed in front of the main hangars and the MB, Sqn Ldr J. M. Dennis, directed the weight of the attack onto them. The results were very concentrated, with the target left shrouded in smoke, and a large fuel explosion caused fires across the airfield. Despite the attack appearing to be a great success, it was only supposed to have taken three minutes from start to finish. Rather than showering his crews with praise, Bennett hauled in the four crews who were late over the target and even went to the length of publishing the code letter of the slowest crew in 8 Group's monthly report. Four Lancasters were lost, one from 35 Squadron, one from 405 Squadron and two from 582 Squadron. Only one airman survived from the 28 aircrew posted missing. Fg Off J. B. Armstrong RCAF managed to evade capture after his aircraft, Lancaster Mk III ND910, was shot down by a night-fighter.

Another good attack was carried out on another airfield on 7/8 May, this time at Nantes. The Master Bomber, Sqn Ldr E. K. Creswell and his experienced deputy, Sqn Ldr E. J. Chigley, orchestrated another accurate attack. A tight group of TIs were dropped between some airfield buildings and a small factory, and although only 93 Lancasters were involved, the bombing was devastating. The dense smoke that immediately rose from the target forced all fourteen of 156 Squadron's Lancasters taking part to bomb on the markers, after initially being ordered to bomb visually. At least six large explosions took place after the bombing had stopped and the fires could be seen over 50 miles away from the target.

The same night saw the first of 3,258 sorties flown against coastal batteries from the Brest peninsular to Scheldt. The campaign opened on Saint-Valery, with 56 Halifaxes from 6 Group, led by 8 PFF Mosquitoes. On this occasion the target was just missed but all did return safely.

No.8 Group were involved in another four operations in a single night on 8/9 May, with a variety of targets being visited. It was a mixed evening of success and failure, with the railway yards and locomotive sheds at Haine-St-Pierre taking a pounding with the help of 6 Group's Halifaxes. A small formation of 31 Halifaxes from 4 Group led by eight PFF Mosquitoes managed to score a direct hit on a coastal gun position at Morsalines. However, 32 Halifaxes from the same group, led by seven PFF Mosquitoes, achieved a different result with only one bomber hitting the target and the majority of bombs falling between 600 and 700 yards from the target. It was similar story with the attack on a gun position at Cap Griz Nez where 30 Lancasters of 3 Group, led by eight PFF Mosquitoes, recorded no hits at all.

No.8 Group now settled into a lengthy period of bombing coastal batteries and rail targets, while the LNSF continued to probe into Germany, keeping the defences

No. 635 Squadron Lancaster ND898 'K for King' parked in the Oak Woods dispersal at Downham Market in late 1944. The bomber is displaying 27 operation symbols under the cockpit. (via Author)

Lancasters of 405
'Vancouver' Squadron
en route to a
target in 1944.
(www.ww2images.com)

on their toes. Mosquitoes of 8 Group were used for a special mine-laying operation for the first time on 12/13 May. Intelligence reports had suggested that the flak defences had been removed from parts of the canal, making a low-level operation possible. In all, 22 Mosquitoes took part and successfully laid their mines where they were supposed to, at the expense of one aircraft from 692 Squadron. Mosquito IV DZ638 being flown by Plt Off D. M. T. Burnett RCAF and Plt Off G. W. Hume is believed to have been shot down by a night-fighter; one of two Mosquitoes lost from 8 Group this night.

The night of 19/20 May was possibly one of the busiest for 8 Group since their formation. The group was involved in eight out of nine different operations being flown, seven of them over northern France and one over Germany. First was Boulogne, where 143 bombers from 4 and 8 Groups attacked the rail yards and, despite only one *Oboe* Mosquito being able to mark, the bombing was accurate. Another accurate raid was Orléans, where 118 Lancasters and four Mosquitoes from 1 and 8 Groups bombed the rail yards. The attack on Amiens was scuppered by the weather and was called off by the MB after 37 of the 112 Lancasters had bombed.

The most successful attack of the night was another rail target, this time at Le Mans, when 112 Lancasters and four Mosquitoes from 3 and 8 Groups, were controlled by MB Wg Cdr J. F. Barron DSO*, DFC, DFM and Sqn Ldr J. M. Dennis DSO, DFC as his deputy. The bulk of the bombing fell within the confines of the rail yard, causing serious damage. This included the destruction of the locomotive sheds and an ammunition train. Both main lines were destroyed and others were disrupted as overhead wires fell across them. Five Lancasters were lost on this operation, including two from 7 Squadron. Sadly, they were Wg Cdr Barron and Sqn Ldr Dennis and their crews. One source claimed they were brought down by light flak while another states that they collided over the target. Whatever occurred that night, 8 Group lost two very talented pilots, along with thirteen experienced aircrew.

Six PFF Mosquitoes led 58 Halifaxes of 6 Group in an attack on a coastal gun position at Le Clipon but could not confirm or deny whether the target was hit because of haze. The other gun position attack that night was against a battery at Merville. The 63 Halifaxes, Lancasters and Mosquitoes taking part from 6 and 8 Groups, only claimed that some bombs did fall on the battery.

The final operation of the evening was another D-Day preparation attack, this time involving the many radar and W/T stations stretching along the coast of northern France. There were actually 66 of them from Dunkirk to Brest and before D-Day, 42 of them would be destroyed. Bomber Command this night were only interested with four: those at Au Fevre, Berneval-le-Grand, Mont Couple and Ferme

D'Urville. A total of 39 Lancasters and five Mosquitoes attacked the radar station at Mont Couple this night. Two *Oboe* Mosquitoes failed to mark the target because of equipment failure but those Lancasters carrying H2S equipment did a timed run from Cap Gris Nez and dropped a tight group of markers for the rest of the formation to bomb. Mont Couple had over 60 transmitters within the complex and after a second attack on 31 May the site was obliterated; officially, described as 'rendered completely unserviceable'.

Harris took every opportunity to continue operations over Germany and the growing numbers of LNSF Mosquitoes made this all the more easy. On 20/21 May, 30 of them attacked Dusseldorf although the target was cloud-covered, with *Oboe* markers disappearing when they were dropped through it. The following night a much bigger force of 510 Lancasters and 22 Mosquitoes from 1, 3, 5 and 8 Groups carried out the first big raid on Duisburg for almost a year. Despite the target being cloud-covered, the *Oboe* sky-marking was accurate and a great deal of damage, including 350 buildings destroyed, was inflicted on the southern part of the city. No. 8 Group lost four Lancasters from the 29 bombers lost, including two from 156 Squadron. One of these, Lancaster Mk III JB217, flown by Flt Sgt V. D. Temple, was attacked by a Ju88 after leaving the target, wounding the mid-upper gunner, Sgt L. E. Reynolds. An Me110 then attempted to finish off the Lancaster but the combined stoic defence put up by Reynolds and the rear gunner, Sgt W. V. Cooper, saw the fighter off. Temple then carried out a forced landing at Dunsfold without further injury to his crew.

One of the most important airfields in north-west France was attacked by 78 Lancasters and five Mosquitoes on 27/28 May. Three out of the five Mosquitoes marked Rennes with *Musical* markers, one of which was planted directly on the A/P. The marking was so good that crews later reported that they could see individual buildings, which was a blessing, as none of 35 Squadron's crews claimed to have heard the MB; and 405 Squadron later stated that all they could hear was a woman's voice jamming the VHF. The bombing was highly concentrated and smoke, dust and fire spread itself across the airfield's buildings. A direct hit on the ammunition dump caused a huge explosion which sadly coincided with the loss of the Deputy MB, Sqn Ldr H. W. B. Heney DSO, RNZAF. Heney was reinforcing the TIs at the time, in Lancaster III ND814 of 582 Squadron, when the bomber was seen to explode. Heney was one of the most experienced PFF pilots, with 59 operations under his belt.

June 1944 – *Overlord* and the Flying-bomb

Ferme-D'Urville radio-listening station, positioned right in the middle of the forthcoming invasion of Normandy, was paid a visit by 101 Halifaxes of 4 Group, led by 8 PFF Mosquitoes. Cloud and haze prevented accurate bombing but a return visit on 3/4 June by 96 Lancasters from 5 Group, led by four PFF Mosquitoes, saw the station wiped off the map. A similar fate befell the radar-jamming station at Berneval on 2/3 June, when 103 Lancasters from 1 Group and four Mosquitoes from 8 Group bombed with excellent accuracy.

While the radio stations were being finished off, the coastal battery campaign continued, including a change of direction to targets in the Pas de Calais area. The attack, by 271 aircraft, was part of the invasion deception plan and, on 2/3 June, four batteries were attacked. The attacks on the Pas de Calais continued on 3/4 June, with Calais and Wimereux being hit hard by 127 Lancasters and 8 Mosquitoes from 1, 3, and 8 Groups. The deception continued on 4/5 June, with four more coastal batteries attacked although, on this occasion, one of them was at Maisy in Normandy. Within 36 hours this would be between *Omaha* and *Utah* beaches. Frustratingly, Maisy was cloud-covered and had to be marked using *Oboe* sky-markers which were bombed by 52 Lancasters from 5 Group.

The activities did not begin for 8 Group until briefings began at 1815 hrs, by which time 'rumour control' was rife that the invasion was on. The word 'invasion' was never mentioned, but the importance placed upon the targets that night and the fact that 1,211 aircraft were detailed to fly, made everyone involved convinced that this was the 'big show'. This was reiterated, when part of the brief was that no aircraft would fly below 6,500 ft, no aircraft was to use IFF (Identification Friend or Foe) and no bombs were to be jettisoned into the Channel.

The evening's sorties for Bomber Command were divided into three major groups: Normandy coastal batteries, support operations and diversion operations. The biggest by far of the three and the one which 8 Group would take part in was the coastal batteries which, by now, was under the name Operation *Flashlamp*. The operation called for 100 bombers to attack ten batteries at La Pernelle, Fontenay, St Martin-de-Varreville, Maisy, Pointe-du-Hoc, Longues, Mont Fleury, Ouistreham, Merville-Franceville and Houlgate. Unfortunately, eight of these crucial batteries were covered in cloud and the bombing was carried out on *Oboe* marking. In total, 946 bombers managed to bomb, dropping almost 5,000 tons of bombs, a record for a single operation since the beginning of the war. Only four bombers were lost on these operations, one of them from 8 Group. By the end of the night, Bomber Command had flown its biggest number of sorties, with a loss of just eight aircraft, equating to 0.7%.

Once the invasion began, most of 8 Group's time was occupied bombing communication targets behind the Normandy battle area. Some 1,065 aircraft

No.405 Squadron crew at Gransden Lodge (from left to right): Bill Hamblin, Johnny Ross, Don Vockins, Tom Downey, Bernard Smoker, Howie Marcon, Eric Bolland and Ron Noice. (www.ww2images.com)

attacked rail and road centres close to French towns, including Achères, Argentan, Caen, Châteaudun, Condé-sur-Noireau, Coutances, St Lô, Lisieux and Vire. One particularly important target was at Forêt De Cerisy on 7/8 June. A total of 112 Lancasters and ten Mosquitoes from 1, 5 and 8 Groups clinically bombed the six-way road junction which was only 2 km away from the nearest village. More importantly for the Allies, the surrounding woods were supposed to contain a fuel dump and at least one tank unit being held in reserve for a counter-attack.

Similar communications raids continued on 9/10 June but the following night, the targets were four Luftwaffe airfields. The targets were Flers, Le Mans, Laval and Rennes, all positioned south of the battle area and it was thought that their destruction could prevent reinforcements being flown closer to the front. All the attacks were successful, especially the one on Rennes which was controlled by MB, Sqn Ldr Creswell and his Deputy Flt Lt G. F. Lambert. Creswell ordered his PFF crews to come down to 6,000 ft. This was below the cloud base and, under the guidance of Creswell and Lambert, the Mosquitoes dropped yellow TIs onto the A/P. The airfield was left shrouded in smoke and, as the formation left the target, a succession of secondary explosions were German fighters on the ground exploding.

The weather had not been kind during the opening days of *Overlord* and a great deal of damage had been caused to the Mulberry harbours. The same storms and very heavy seas had forced a small but very dangerous fleet of enemy vessels, including several E-boats, to take shelter in Le Havre. Their presence, so close to the supply lines, made the Allied commanders very nervous and the only solution lay with Bomber Command. Harris was equally nervous about sending his crews out in daylight, but for this attack, Spitfires from 11 Group could escort the bombers all the way to the target. On the evening of 14 June, 221 Lancasters and thirteen Mosquitoes from 1, 3, 5 and 8 Groups began the first daylight operation since 2 Group left the command in May 1943. The attack took place in two waves: the first bombed the harbour in the early evening. The naval area of the port was devastated because of controlled *Oboe* marking, including a particularly accurate attack led by 8 Group Mosquitoes for 617 Squadron, who dropped 12,000 lb Tallboys directly onto the E-boat pens. By the time the second wave arrived over Le Havre at dusk, the port was well ablaze. The threat of attack from the sea was removed in this single, effective raid and at least fourteen E-boats, three R-boats, three torpedo boats and fifteen auxiliary ships were destroyed, as well as over 1,000 marines killed. A similar, successful attack took place on Boulogne the following evening.

Britain had been aware from 1939 that Hitler had been investing a great deal of time and effort into developing rockets. Both Peenemünde and, not long after, Watten, were attacked by Bomber Command and the USAAF but it was not until December 1943 that the connection had been made between the structures appearing in the Pas de Calais and 'V' weapons. These sites were then attacked by *Oboe* Mosquitoes making the Germans realise, very quickly, the vulnerability of such structures from the air and so they set about developing smaller, more mobile, launchers. The first of these was spotted at Belhamelin in the Cherbourg peninsular on 26 April, 1944. However, the Allied air forces were so pre-occupied with supporting *Overlord* that the mobile launching sites slipped down the priority list until 13 June. On this day, at 0418 hrs the first of approximately 10,000 V-1s launched at Britain came down at Swanscombe, near Gravesend. This single act saw the war on the V-1 rise up the priority list and was only surpassed by the 'absolute' needs of *Overlord*.

The first of many heavy attacks on flying-bomb sites began on 16/17 June when 405 Lancasters, Halifaxes and Mosquitoes bombed four targets in the Pas de Calais area. All were marked by *Oboe* Mosquitoes and all four were claimed as destroyed without loss. Attacks on flying-bombs would continue in strength until the end of August 1944 and, at first, losses were few, as the sites were lightly defended and fighters were not in abundance over the area. This changed on 23/24 June when 412 Lancasters, Halifaxes and Mosquitoes set out to attack another quartet of flying-bomb sites. The enemy fighter controllers quickly got wise to Bomber Command's targets and this night began sending night-fighters westwards rather than holding them back. Only five Lancasters were lost but, unfortunately, they all came from 8 Group. Many more survived close encounters with enemy night-fighters and at least one was shot down, including the Deputy Master Bomber, Flt Lt B. G. Frow during an attack on L'Hey. At 0025 hrs, the Lancaster ahead of Frow suddenly came under attack from a Ju88. Fg Off K. Milligan, the bomb-aimer was already in the front turret and Frow gave him permission to fire which, combined with the weight of fire from W/O O. G. Erasmus, forced the fighter to break off. Only minutes later, the rear gunner, Flt Lt E. Wharton spotted an unknown night-fighter closing to attack. Without hesitation, Wharton opened fire, hitting the fighter in the starboard engine and forcing it to dive away steeply before exploding. This was not the last of it for the Frow crew who, while frantically trying to clear stoppages, were attacked by an Me210. The twin-engined fighter attacked from below, hitting the Lancaster in the mainplane, tailplane, fin and rudder. However, the enemy made the mistake of coming back to finish the bomber off and by now Wharton and Erasmus had cleared their guns. Before the Me210 had chance to fire, both turrets opened up and the fighter dived away as machine-gun bullets tore into it. Frow later made an emergency landing at Woodbridge, with injury to his crew.

A classic example of precision bombing took place in daylight on 30 June at Villers-Bocage. The target was a road junction through which the 2nd and 9th Panzer Divisions were planning on attacking the Allies that evening. A force of 266 aircraft from 3, 4 and 8 Groups were carefully controlled by the MB, who ordered

Although this is a 5 Group scene at Coningsby in 1944, the 250 lb Yellow Target Indicators being loaded aboard the Mosquito were standard for 8 Group as well. (Mike Garbett and Brian Goulding collection)

A sad scene at Downham Market; the owners of this Wolseley Datona, MG Sports, Morris 8 and Panther have been declared as missing, and most likely will never see their beloved cars again. (via Author)

them to descend to as low as 4,000 ft, to make sure that they bombed on the markers. In total, 1,100 tons of bombs were accurately dropped and the planned Panzer attack never came to fruition.

July 1944 – 'Heavy *Oboe*' Attack Method

Flying-bomb sites continued to dominate the first few days of July as it had during June. On 7 July, Bomber Command was rallied again in support of the troops on the ground, this time against an area north of Caen. Some 467 aircraft from 1, 4, 6 and 8 Group, led by MB, Wg Cdr S. P. Daniels of 35 Squadron, were tasked with attacking a series of strongholds north of Caen which were holding up the Canadian

The Merlin 85 and 87 powered Lancaster Mk VIs were tentatively introduced to
8 Group during 1944. This JB675, the Mk VI prototype, briefly saw service
with 7, 405 and 635 Squadrons before being returned to Rolls-Royce.
(via Author)

1st Army and the British 2nd Army. The strongholds were actually within several villages which were close to Allied troops and this proximity forced the bombers to attack an area slightly further back towards Caen. The bombing was, once again, very accurate but few enemy troops were killed despite 2,276 tons of bombs being dropped. Only one 8 Group aircraft was lost, 105 Squadron Mosquito XVI ML964 being flown by Sqn Ldr W. Blessing DSO, DFC, RAAF and Plt Off D. T. Burke. Acting as one of the PTMs, the Mosquito was mauled by an enemy fighter and, after Burke bailed out safely, Blessing lost control and crashed behind Allied lines.

Another new technique, known as 'heavy *Oboe*', was introduced by 8 Group on 11 July. The raid only involved six Mosquitoes and 26 Lancasters, one of which, a 582 Squadron machine, was fitted with *Oboe* equipment and flown by Wg Cdr G.

Mosquito IVs of 139 Squadron at Marham prepare to depart on another operation. Nearest to the camera is DZ421, which was lost after take-off on a NAVEX with 1655 MTU on 25 July 1944. Next to it is DZ373, which went missing on an operation to Liège, not long after this photograph was taken on 12 March 1943. (www.ww2images.com)

Sqn Ldr A. Cranswick DSO, DFC, who was killed serving with 35 Squadron, over Villeneuve St George on 4/5 July 1944, having flown 104 operations with 8 Group. (Mike Garbett and Brian Goulding collection)

F. Grant from 109 Squadron. Grant directed the raid on a flying bomb site at Gapennes from his Lancaster and when he released his bombs, the other Lancasters in the formation did the same. The method dropped a greater tonnage of bombs on *Oboe* signals than had been achieved before and the technique went on to become one of Bomber Command's most accurate ways of bombing a small target.

Various communications, supply dumps and flying-bomb sites were the regular targets up to 18 July when Bomber Command was asked to attack the bottleneck north of Caen again. The attack had to be successful this time as the Allies were about to unleash Operation *Goodwood* which would, hopefully, punch through the German lines and beyond. Shortly before the second raid of 942 aircraft began, the Allied infantry quietly withdrew from their positions. Once again, the objective was five fortified villages and, on this occasion, they were bombed directly, four of them having been successfully marked by *Oboe*. For the fifth village, the MB, Sqn Ldr E. K. Creswell and other 8 Groups bombed visually and, by the time the attack was over, Bomber Command had dropped 5,000 tons of bombs. The USAAF also dropped a further 1,800 tons of bombs accompanied by Allied artillery. The raid that day has been described as the best carried out by Bomber Command in support of the Allied forces.

As the month progressed, forays into Germany began to increase again and, on 23/24 July, a new campaign against oil targets in the occupied countries began. First was an oil refinery at Donges, close to the mouth of the River Loire. A total of 119 aircraft took part: 100 Halifaxes, fourteen Lancasters and five Mosquitoes from 6 and 8 Groups. The raid was a success and, as well as severe damage to the refinery, a tanker was also sunk in the river.

August 1944 – 8 Group's first Victoria Cross

Downham Market gained a second squadron on 1 August and another Mosquito unit for the Group. No. 608 (North Riding) Squadron, which was originally formed at Thornaby in 1930 as part of the Auxiliary Air Force, was re-formed at Downham Market with the Mosquito XX. The unit was destined to remain at its Norfolk home until it was disbanded in August 1945.

The month began as the previous had ended, with more attacks on flying-bomb and storage sites, all of which were generally successful. Almost seen as routine operations by this time, one in particular stands out above the rest, because of the actions of one 635 Squadron pilot on 4 August.

The attack was against the flying-bomb storage sites at Bois de Cassan and Trossy-St-Maxim, and involved 291 aircraft from 6 and 8 Groups. The site at Trossy

'Omnibus ungulis' (With all talons) was the motto of 608 (North Riding) Squadron, which was re-formed in 8 Group at Downham Market on 1 August 1944, with Mosquitoes. (via Author)

had only been bombed a few days earlier and the local flak crews were more than ready if Bomber Command dared to return. A total of 61 Lancasters from 8 Group, led by MB, Wg Cdr D. W. S. Clark, had a rough ride on approaching the site and, of the 14 crews from 635 Squadron taking part, eight were damaged by flak before a bomb was dropped. The first of two 635 Squadron Lancasters shot down that day was being flown by Flt Lt R. W. Beveridge DFC. His aircraft, Lancaster III PA983, took a direct flak hit, burst into flames and nose-dived into the ground near the target, killing all eight on board.

The second 635 Squadron Lancaster lost belonged to Sqn Ldr I. W. Bazalgette whose aircraft Mk III ND811 was hit by a barrage of heavy flak as he neared the target. Both starboard engines were knocked out and the starboard wing and fuselage were set on fire. His bomb-aimer, Flt Lt I. A. Hibbert DFC, was seriously injured but Bazalgette continued on while his crew tried to put out the fires. After dropping his bombs, the Lancaster entered a spin, but Bazalgette managed to regain control while the fire in the main plane would not subside. The seriously-damaged bomber flew on for another 30 miles before a port engine seized, giving Bazalgette no choice but to order 'abandon aircraft'. His crew were more concerned with the health of Hibbert and the mid-upper gunner, Flt Sgt V. V. R. Leeder, who had been overcome by fumes. Bazalgette assured them that he would attempt to crash land and four of his crew bailed out safely at 1,000 ft.

Sqn Ldr I. W. Bazalgette of 635 Squadron, who was 8 Group's first recipient of the Victoria Cross, for his actions over Trossy-St-Maxim, on 4 August 1944. (via Author)

It was at this point that the people of the French village of Senantes saw the burning bomber approaching. The Lancaster then veered away, as if to avoid the village, before Bazalgette carried out an excellent crash-landing in a nearby field. All seemed well until, seconds later, the bomber exploded, killing the three airmen still on board instantly. The whole village turned out to honour Bazalgette, Hibbert and Leeder and the Mayor of Senantes wrote a letter of sympathy to the pilot's mother.

When the crew arrived back in England, the story of Bazalgette's final flight was told and the brave pilot was awarded the highest accolade, the Victoria Cross, the first one earned by a member of 8 Group.

On the night of 10/11 August, as part of several minor operations, three 8 Group Lancasters with a difference set out to bomb Bremen. The aircraft was the Mk VI, fitted with a set of Merlin 85/87 engines which were tuned for much improved high-altitude performance. It is not clear which unit the three bombers were allocated to but of the nine Mk VIs that were converted from Mk IIIs all served with the PFF on

A very rare photo of Lancaster VI ND673, still wearing the striped fins applied during its brief service with 635 Squadron. (www.ww2images.com)

7, 83, 405 and 635 Squadrons. The increased performance of the Mk VI allowed the bomber to carry and drop the first 10,000 lb GP bombs on Bremen, the first time such a weapon had seen service with Bomber Command.

The dangers of close-quarter tactical bombing were clearly displayed on 14 August when 805 aircraft were sent to attack seven separate targets in front of the 3rd Canadian Division. The targets were carefully planned, with a combined *Oboe* and visual marking approach under the control of an MB and DMB (Deputy Master Bomber) for each individual target. The majority of the bombing was accurate. However, halfway through the raid, several aircraft began bombing a quarry where elements of the 12th Canadian Field Regiment were positioned. Unfortunately, the Canadians were using yellow indication flares which were similar

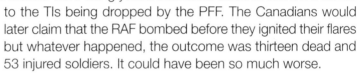

to the TIs being dropped by the PFF. The Canadians would later claim that the RAF bombed before they ignited their flares but whatever happened, the outcome was thirteen dead and 53 injured soldiers. It could have been so much worse.

Bomber Command had not played a particularly large role in the destruction of enemy airfields but on 15 August, 1,004 bombers were detailed to attack nine Luftwaffe night-fighter airfields in Belgium and Holland. With Spitfires flying as escort on a beautiful summer's day, all the targets were marked by the PFF by Controlled Visual method and all were bombed heavily. Only three bombers were lost, none of them from 8 Group, although this would change as Arthur Harris prepared to resume his attacks on Germany.

From mid-August, attacks against German towns and cities were back on the agenda with Stettin, Kiel, Bremen, Rüsselsheim and Darmstadt all receiving a visit. The end of a successful campaign against the V-1 menace, with a 150-aircraft attack on several launching and storage sites in the Pas de Calais region, was marked on 28 August. No. 8 Group Mosquitoes carried out an excellent '*Oboe* -leader' raid on twelve targets, the majority of which were sufficiently damaged or destroyed.

September 1944 – Operation *Market Garden*

Following a successful pair of raids on the V-2 rocket stores at Lumbres and La Pourchinte on 1 September, a second attack

Bombing photo taken from Sqn Ldr Wesselow's 635 Squadron Lancaster on an 872 aircraft raid to Calais on 25 September 1944. Note the Halifaxes below, some of the 397 taking part. (www.ww2images.com)

on Luftwaffe airfields was organised two days later. A total of 675 aircraft carried out heavy attacks on six airfields in southern Holland, without loss to the PFF.

Le Havre proved to be another bottleneck for the advancing Allies during early September but a bombing campaign from the 5th to the 11th of the month saw the 11,300-strong garrison surrender, despite Hitler ordering their commander, Col Eberard Wildemuth, to fight to the last man.

A force of 348 aircraft from 1, 3 and 8 Groups began the Le Havre campaign with a very heavy raid without loss. Another 333 aircraft attacked the port again on 8 September on a raid which had five A/Ps. However, on arrival, Le Havre was 7–8/10ths cloud-covered, with a base that extended from 1,000 to 4,000 ft and terminated at 8,000 ft. Wg Cdr H. A. Morrison RCAF of 405 Squadron, caught sight of the *Oboe* TIs on the third A/P and ordered the crews to orbit until they reached the cloud base. Morrison made three orbits and did not break cloud until he was at 1,000 ft, making him particularly vulnerable to flak. Three bursts in quick succession removed the starboard aileron, damaged the starboard wing and set it on fire. The aircraft, Lancaster III PA970, became uncontrollable and Morrison gave the order to bail out. All eight crew managed to escape and evade capture, while the bomber plunged onto the beach on the edge of the port. Four Lancasters were lost on this raid; one of them was from 8 Group, Mk III PB123 of 582 Squadron which came down in Le Havre. Only two crew managed to bail out and evade capture.

The following day, another 272 aircraft from 4, 6 and 8 Groups attacked Le Havre again, this time in such poor visibility that the MB abandoned the raid. All aircraft returned safely back to their respective airfields with their bomb loads intact. Unfortunately, at Upwood, while the armourers were removing the bomb load from Lancaster III, ND978, flown by the CO of 156 Squadron, Wg Cdr T. L. Bingham-Hall DFC, disaster struck. The bomb load exploded at 1120 hrs, killing six ground crew and injuring a seventh, as well as destroying ND978 and wrecking nearby Mk III ND618.

No aircraft were lost in another concentrated raid on Le Havre on 10 September, when 992 aircraft attacked eight coastal batteries around the port. The PFF marked the A/Ps which, for the first time, were named after cars. Buick I and II, Alvis I to IV and Bentley I and II were all obliterated and on this raid a new addition to the PFF, the 'Long Stop' was incorporated. As the bombing was close to Allied troops, the MBs and DMBs also had another crew called the 'Long Stop', which could call a halt to the bombing if the marking was off target. On this occasion, the 'Long Stop' was Gp Capt P. H. Cribb and by dropping yellow TIs he gave the raid an additional element of control. The following day, 218 bombers attacked the German positions again but smoke and dust caused by the first wave forced the MB to abandon the raid. Hours later the Germans had had enough.

No.8 Group's Mosquito strength increased again on 15 September, when 128 Squadron was re-formed at Wyton. Initial equipment was the Mosquito XX which was complemented by the Mk XXV and Mk XVI by October. No.128 Squadron operated from Wyton until the end of the war, moving to Warboys on 22 June 1945 and later departing for Germany before the year was over.

No.8 Group's role in support of the ill-fated Operation *Market Garden* was a brief, but important one, which began on the night of 16/17 September prior to the airborne troops landing at Arnhem and Nijmegen. Some 200 Lancasters and 23 Mosquitoes from 1 and 8 Groups attacked airfields at Hopsten, Leeuwarden, Steenwijk and Rheine, while another 54 Lancasters and five Mosquitoes bombed a flak position at Moerdijk. All of the airfield's runways were heavily cratered but the flak position escaped with damage. The following morning, 112 Lancasters and 20 Mosquitoes from 1 and 8 Groups attacked a flak position in the Flushing area, this time successfully.

This was 8 Group's only contribution to *Market Garden* and the remainder of September was dominated by heavy raids in the Calais area, where stubborn German forces were holding out against the Allies.

October 1944 – The second Battle of the Ruhr begins

Released from Eisenhower's control, Arthur Harris was now free to continue his campaign against Germany without distraction. By now, Bomber Command also had complete freedom of the skies and bombing accuracy was on the increase. Experienced crews were also more readily available as the loss rate began to finally subside and many hindsight strategists have wondered why this situation was not exploited more by Harris. Criticized for continuing his area-bombing policy virtually to the war's end, Harris was regularly at loggerheads with the Air Staff and offered to resign on more than one occasion. The Chief of the Air Staff, Sir Charles Portal, could have replaced Harris at any point, but chose to leave the Bomber Command AOC-in-C in place, therefore sharing the blame for any wayward bombing policy.

Area bombing would have eventually broken the German economy but strategists of the day wanted the war over quickly and, to do this, the targets should have been oil and transport. From October to December, 53% of Bomber Command's attacks were against cities, while just 15% were on transport and 14% were on oil targets. These targets did move into the frame more prominently in early 1945 but by now the chance to get to Berlin first had been lost by some margin to the Russians.

The second Battle of the Ruhr began on 6/7 October, with a 523-strong raid,

Lancaster III PB179 'Z' of 582 Squadron is prepared for a raid on Castrop Rauxel on 21/22 November 1944. The Austin Ruby under the wing was owned by the pilot, Fg Off F. Lloyd. (Mike Garbett and Brian Goulding collection)

made up of 3, 6 and 8 Groups on Dortmund. *Oboe* marking was carried out by 105 and 109 Squadron's Mosquitoes, but for the former, only one out of the twelve aircraft involved managed to mark the target. Luckily, the remainder marked the target accurately and severe damage was inflicted to the industrial, transport and residential areas of the city. Five aircraft were lost, including 105 Squadron Mosquito XVI ML996 which was lost without trace.

Another phase of Bomber Command operations began on 14 October, when Operation *Hurricane* began. The directive which was sent to Arthur Harris described *Hurricane* as follows: 'In order to demonstrate to the enemy in Germany generally the over-whelming superiority of the Allied Air Forces in this theatre…' To prove this, Duisburg was selected and, thanks to a 48-hour stand down, Bomber Command could summon 1,013 bombers, which were provided with an RAF fighter escort. A difficult target to obliterate because of its wide open spaces between the built-up areas, the PFF Mosquitoes marked five different A/Ps using *Oboe*. Medium level cloud made it difficult for some crews to see the TIs but 957 bombers still managed to drop 3,574 tons of bombs on the city.

There was no let-up for Duisburg which was also attacked by 1,251 8th Air Force bombers and again by the RAF that evening, with another 1,005 Lancasters, Halifaxes and Mosquitoes. The huge force was treated to excellent marking by the PFF and another 4,040 tons of bombs were dropped on what remained of the city. Incredibly, Bomber Command had flown 2,589 sorties during this 24-hour period which would remain its peak effort for the entire war. With regard to Operation *Hurricane* it was successful in devastating Duisburg but, by this stage of the war, the German people were under no illusion that the Allied Air Forces dominated the sky and, to them, this was just another very heavy raid.

More Mosquitoes were added to 8 Group's LNSF on 25 October when 142 Squadron was re-formed at Gransden Lodge. After service in the First World War, the squadron was re-formed as a bomber unit in June 1934 and, with the exception of the early months, had been operating the Wellington until disbandment came at Regina on 5 October. Re-equipped with the Mosquito XXV, the unit operated solely with 8 Group from Gransden Lodge until it was disbanded on 28 September, 1945.

No.8 Group carried out a *Musical Wanganui* on Cologne on 20/31 October and, by the end of the raid, 3,431 tons of HE and 610 tons of IBs had been dropped. No aircraft were lost and Bomber Command described the raid as 'scattered and light'.

Lancasters of 635 Squadron 'stacking up' for another operation from Downham Market in late 1944. (Mike Garbett and Brian Goulding collection)

JACKSON   PRITCHARD   DAVY   CHESWELL   PALMER   SKITON   CARPENTER   FELLOWES
   FINLAY   GARRATT   POWELL   CURTIS   BRAMELD   LAMBERT   LOCATELLI   SIMPSON
PIZAN   DEAN   BOWLEY   FALKINDER   LENDON   LAW   DOUGLAS   ROSTRON   WRIGHT   FRASER   HOFGART
FRANKLIN   MORGAN   DRAY   WILLIAMSON   DENNANT   BURT   BOND   MOUNTAIN   SANDERS   TRENERRY
   COX   GREENHILL   POWLES   FUNNELL   GILMORE   BROWN   MARRIOTT
BURNETT   ANGOOD   GARNER   PARKIN   BEARDSALL   LAING   ROWLEY   HENDERSON
'A' FLIGHT 109 SQDN – OCT. 1944

'A' Flight, 109 Squadron make time for a formal group photo at Little Staughton in October 1944. The squadron remained at the Cambridgeshire station until their disbandment on 30 April 1945. (via Author)

However, it was a different story on the ground, where the western part of the city had been devastated.

The following evening, 493 aircraft returned to Cologne, made up of aircraft from 1, 3, 4 and 8 Groups. Another good display of *Oboe* marking through cloud was carried out by the PFF Mosquitoes and many crews later commented that it was the best display of sky-marking they had experienced. None of 8 Group's aircraft were lost over Cologne, mainly because of a successful feint by fifteen Mosquitoes just before the raid began.

November 1944 – LNSF attacks grow in strength

Poor weather disrupted operations during November but this did not stop the LNSF from attacking a host of targets, with Hannover, which was bombed nine times, being favoured over Berlin. However, Berlin was still on the cards on 3/4 November,

Nicknamed the 'Mighty Wurlitzer', Flt Sgt F. Kelsh of 635 Squadron demonstrates the Fraser-Nash FN20 rear turret with its four .303 ins Brown machine-guns. (Mike Garbett and Brian Goulding collection)

with 55 Mosquitoes heading for the capital and nine more attacking Herford. The attack was marred by the loss of Mosquito XVI of 128 Squadron which crashed on approach to Wyton after an engine failed.

Oboe-guided raids, thanks to the advancing Allies could now be extended further east, putting cities such as Stuttgart well within range. On 5/6 November, 65

Mosquitoes, led by *Oboe* and backed up by 139 Squadron, hit the city in two phases, 3½ hours apart. Many of the crews involved, all of whom returned safely, reported huge fires and large explosions throughout both phases.

It was not unusual for the LNSF to despatch 60 Mosquitoes at a time but, on 28/29 November, the force excelled itself by sending 75 aircraft to Nuremburg and nine to Hallendorf. Two more Mosquitoes were lost on this successful raid, including W/O F. Edgar and Sgt J. H. M. Murphy RCAF who were lost without trace over Nuremburg in their 128 Squadron Mosquito XVI. The law of averages began to rise for the Mosquitoes, with more of them over the target area than ever before; the losses for November had surpassed 8 Group's Lancaster losses for a second month in a row.

No.5 Group appeared to be more active than 8 Group during November, with attacks on the Dortmund-Elms canal, Trondheim and the final visit to sink the *Tirpitz*. However, two 8 Group led raids which stand out above the rest took place on 28/29

Mosquitoes of 128 Squadron being waved off at dusk, for another operation from Wyton in late 1944. (www.ww2images.com)

November. One involved 341 Lancasters and ten Mosquitoes from 1 and 8 Groups against Freiburg, near the Swiss border and the other, with 290 aircraft from 1, 6 and 8 Groups was to Neuss.

Freiburg had not been attacked by the RAF before but it was believed that German troops were congregating there to take on US and French troops advancing in the Vosges mountains, 35 miles to the west. The attack was possible because the *Oboe* ground crews, operating from mobile caravans in France, could extend the operating range of the system. The ten Mosquitoes involved, five each from 105 and 109 Squadrons, began the raid by accurately dropping the first TIs, aided by Illuminators directly onto the A/P. The attack was expertly led by Wg Cdr T. E. Ison and, despite the 5/10th broken cloud over the target, he managed to convince his crews to exercise a little patience and wait for a clear bombing run. The result, as described by the Germans, was one of the most outstanding attacks of the year. No less than 1,900 tons of bombs were dropped in 25 minutes and because the town was not prepared for an air attack, the civilian population took the brunt of the casualties with 2,008 people killed, compared to just 75 German soldiers.

Over Neuss, the bomber crews had to contend with 10/10th thin stratus but this was overcome by *Oboe* Mosquitoes dropping ground and sky markers, giving crews a choice of bombing on green or red TIs. The bulk of the bombing fell in the central and eastern districts and many fires were started. Compared to Freiburg, Neuss was prepared for air attack, being situated on the edge of the Ruhr. As a result, only 41 people were killed.

December 1944 – 8 Group's only *Oboe* VC

Following raids on Hagen, Heimbach and the steelworks at Hellendorf, 8 Group were given the opportunity to attack a special target on 4 December, normally reserved for a 5 Group squadron. The target was the Urft Dam in the Eifel which the Germans were using to release water to flood areas through which US forces were advancing. Only 27 Lancasters and three Mosquitoes, all from 8 Group, took part in the first of two raids but unfortunately only succeeded in blasting 13 ft off the top of the dam. On 11 December, 233 Lancasters from 5 Group, led by five Mosquitoes of 8 Group, tried to make a better job of it, but once again, the dam was hit but not breached. There really was only one way to breach a German dam and that was partially achieved in May 1943.

The penultimate unit to join 8 Group arrived at Bourn on 16 December, 1944. Originally formed in January 1942 at Kabrit from a detachment from 109 Squadron, 162 Squadron was a bomber unit which operated the Wellington, Blenheim,

Baltimore and, briefly, the Mosquito VI. Disbanded at Idku on 25 September, the squadron was re-formed as part of 8 Group's LNSF, operating the Mosquito XXV and from February 1945, the Mosquito XX as well. The squadron was destined to lose just one aircraft in action, the lowest of all 8 Group units, before being transferred to Transport Command on 10 July, 1945.

On the morning of 23 December, a small force of 27 Lancasters and three Mosquitoes from 8 Group left Bourn, Graveley and Little Staughton to attack the Gremberg marshalling yards in Cologne. The aircraft were divided into three formations, each led by an *Oboe* Lancaster, with an *Oboe* Mosquito flying close behind in reserve. The raid did not get off to a good start as two 35 Squadron

The famous 105 and 109 Squadron Mosquito IV LR503, more commonly known as 'F for Freddie' captured after completing its 203rd sortie. The 'Mossie' went on to complete 213 operations, the last being flown to the rail yards at Leipzig on 10 April 1945. (Howard Lees via Author)

Nice snapshot, (which was not allowed to be taken!) by Harry Wright of 582 Squadron of a Lancaster and the night's bomb load, being delivered at Little Staughton. (Harry Wright via www.ww2images.com)

Sqn Ldr Robert Anthony Maurice Palmer DFC who was posthumously awarded the Victoria Cross for his actions on 23 December 1944. (via Author)

Lancasters, PB678 and PB683, collided at 10,000 ft while over South Foreland, off the Kent coast. All fourteen aircrew were lost although it is claimed that some managed to escape by parachute into the sea, but died of exposure before help arrived.

Once the remaining 28 aircraft reached the target, the forecasted cloud over Cologne had cleared and, rather than risking a long *Oboe* run in, all aircraft were ordered to break formation and bomb visually. Flying at just 17,000 ft, the flak began to take its toll but the lead aircraft, 582 Squadron Lancaster III PB371, was being flown by MB Sqn Ldr R. A. M. Palmer DFC & Bar (on loan from 109 Squadron). Palmer, on his 110th sortie, failed to receive the break formation order and continued on the planned *Oboe* course to the target. Flak tore into Palmer's aircraft, setting two engines on fire and flames quickly spread through the fuselage, setting the bomb-bay ablaze. Palmer knew that during this type of attack, the formation only released their bombs when the lead aircraft did. Maintaining his course, Palmer released his bombs when the signal was received from the ground station and his bombs were seen to land on the marshalling yards. Seconds later, Palmer lost control and PB371 spiralled into the target area. Only the rear gunner, Flt Sgt R. K. Yeulatt RCAF, managed to bail out to become a POW. Behind Palmer's aircraft was Fg Off E. C. Carpenter RCAF and Fg Off W. T. Lambeth DFM in 109 Squadron Mosquito XVI ML998. With one engine feathered, Carpenter had four enemy fighters on his tail but knew that he could not drop his bombs early. After dropping its bombs, ML998 also spiralled down in flames; neither aircrew escaped with their lives.

The 8 Group formation found themselves up against part of a force of 250 German fighters which had been sent to the area to attack an 8th Air Force raid. Before the action was over, three more Lancasters had been shot down, all from 582 Squadron, with the loss of another nine air crew although twelve survived to become POWs. Two of those POWs were Fg Off H. E. Parratt DFM and Flt Sgt R. K. Shirley who were trapped in Lancaster III, PB141 after it entered a flat spin at 20,000 ft and crashed into the marshalling yard they were bombing.

Several other bombers were damaged by flak and shot up by fighters, including those belonging to Wg Cdr J. H. Clough and Capt E. Swales, who both had running battles with Fw190s and Bf109s. But the day went to Sqn Ldr Palmer who was awarded the highest accolade, a posthumous VC, becoming the only *Oboe* VC of the Second World War. He lies in Rheinberg War Cemetery alongside his crew.

Operations

1945

January 1945 – the Mosquito takes charge

New Year's Day 1945 saw a classic example of 8 Group's Mosquitoes in action when seventeen of them attacked railway tunnels between the Rhine and the Ardennes battle area. The object of the exercise was to prevent German forces from being reinforced. In broad daylight and with a 'cookie' apiece, the Mosquitoes dived to 200 ft, dropping their short-fuse delay bombs into the entrances of the tunnels. One crew, Plt D. R. Tucker and Sgt F. A. J. David, of 571 Squadron, found three tunnels and, after making a dummy run on each, in full view of the local villagers, dropped their cookie perfectly into the entrance. Tucker banked round to view his handy work and saw that the whole tunnel had erupted, causing the hillside to collapse into the path of an approaching train.

The long midwinter nights also gave the LNSF an opportunity to fly two sorties per evening with two crews and the same aircraft. On 4/5 January, several 8 Group Mosquitoes attacked Berlin after taking off in the early evening, returning, changing crews and attacking the German capital again before returning back to their home bases before the sun rose.

Sir Arthur Harris faced a great deal of criticism for not concentrating his forces on the Wehrmacht's oil supplies during late 1944. In his defence, 23,000 tons of bombs were dropped on such targets, which was half the total of all bombs dropped on Germany during 1943. No.8 Group was mainly interested in the oil plants in the Ruhr which were capable of producing one third of all of Germany's needs. By late November, the Ruhr plants were virtually at a standstill and the focus of attention was now the main plants outside the Ruhr at Brux, Leuna and Politz. Leuna, Germany's largest synthetic oil plant, was singled out for a two-phase attack on 14/15 January, involving 573 Lancasters and 14 Mosquitoes from 1, 5, 6 and 8 Groups. The MB of the second phase of the raid, Sqn Ldr C. P. C. de Wesselow, found the target covered by 10/10th low stratus at 2,000 ft. There was also very little evidence that the 200-strong first phase had hit the target although a few small fires were reported by crews further north from the target.

The conditions called for *Wanganui* flares and as the winds were light at 15,000 ft, they only drifted slowly which contributed to a display of concentrated bombing. (It was the norm for *Wanganui* flares to be fused to burst at between 15,000 and 16,000ft.) As the first bombs began to fall on the oil plant, two large explosions started raging fires which belched thick black smoke that quickly rose above the dense stratus, giving the crews another unplanned target marker. The raid was an outstanding success for the PFF, the northern half of the plant being particularly heavily hit and a host of vital components were destroyed, putting Leuna out of action until the end of the war. Twelve Lancasters were lost, none of them from 8 Group although at least two bombers were hit by 'friendly' bombs over the target. One proved fatal for the rear gunner of Sqn Ldr D. B. Everett's 35 Squadron Lancaster when Fg Off R. T. Salvoni's turret was severed by a falling bomb, sending him plunging to his death. The mid-upper gunner of another 8 Group Lancaster had a very lucky escape when two bombs crashed through the fuselage just ahead of his turret. The pilot, Fg Off F. Lloyd, lost control of the damaged bomber and ordered his crew to bail out. However, the G-forces prevented only the bomb-aimer from leaving. By the time the Lancaster was down to 10,000 ft, Lloyd was back in control and rescinded his earlier order. After a struggle across the North Sea on two engines, Lloyd managed to land his aircraft safely at Manston. The remainder of 8 Group's aircraft were all diverted to Ford and Exeter as their home airfields were closed because of poor weather.

The final piece of the 8 Group Mosquito jigsaw was in place on 25 January, 1945 when 163 Squadron was reformed at Wyton. Originally formed at Suez in July 1942 with the Hudson, by December of that year, the unit only existed as a cadre. Re-equipped with the Mosquito XXV, this mark was replaced by the XVI in May 1945, which saw very action before the war's end. This short-lived but useful contribution to 8 Group was disbanded on 10 August, 1945. No. 163 Squadron's arrival now meant that Bennett could easily muster 150 Mosquitoes at a moment's notice without putting up maximum effort.

February 1945 – Bomber Command's last VC of the war

The ever-increasing Mosquito strength was put to good effect on 1/2 February, 1945 when 176 Mosquito sorties were flown on eight separate targets. Ludwigshafen, Mainz, Siegen, Bruckhausen, Hannover, Nuremburg and Berlin were all hit; the latter involving 122 Mosquitoes. Berlin would suffer mercilessly at the hands of the LNSF during the final months of the war and, from 20/21 February, the

Mosquito XVI ML963 of 571 Squadron, showing off her best lines to renowned aviation photographer Charles E. Brown. (C. E. Brown, via Author)

capital was attacked on 36 consecutive nights. Averaging 60 Mosquitoes per raid, 2,538 sorties were flown to Berlin, of which 2,409 were successful. Some 855 cookies were dropped on the city during this period alone and the LNSF continued to bomb Berlin right up to the arrival of the Russian forces in late April 1945.

Pforzheim was almost wiped off the map on 23/24 February when it was bombed by 367 Lancasters and thirteen Mosquitoes from 1, 6 and 8 Groups for the first and last time. The raid was led by MB, Capt E. Swales DFC, SAAF (the only member of the SAAF to serve with the PFF), and a new method was used in an attempt to draw away enemy night-fighters from the main force. The attack was a Controlled *Musical Parramatta* at low level and a *Mandrel* screen was used to cover a *Window* spoof. The Main Force approached the target at just 5,000 ft until it reached 07°00E (over Saarbrücken) and then climbed to 8,000 ft, on track for Pforzheim. Despite the spoofing and different approach to the target, a large formation of enemy night-fighters was already congregating over Stuttgart and they would make their presence felt.

The MB, his deputy and two PVMs easily identified the A/P with the help of Blind Illuminators' flares which were dropped accurately around TIs positioned by *Oboe*. The PFF then quickly dropped an excellent concentration of reds and greens. The Main Force then followed up with an excellent piece of bombing which saw 1,825 tons of bombs fall within 22 minutes, devastating over 80% of the town. It is believed that 17,600 people were killed, the majority in a firestorm which erased an area of the town measuring 3 km by 1½ km. The death toll was only surpassed by Hamburg and Dresden during the entire war.

For the attackers, ten Lancasters were shot down and two more crashed in France; one of the latter was from 8 Group. The PFF only lost one bomber this night, namely that of the MB, Capt Swales, in Lancaster III PB538 of 582 Squadron. Just eight minutes after dropping his TIs and while still controlling the raid, Swales' Lancaster was attacked by an Me410 flown by Hptm G. Friedrich of II./NJG1. The fighter was spotted first by the rear gunner, Plt Off N. Bourne RCAF who lost sight of it before spotting it again climbing towards PB538 to attack. Bourne called for Swales to dive to starboard, but the message never got through and the Me410 opened fire at 800 yards while the rear gunner returned fire. Bourne saw his tracer hit the night-fighter but Friedrich continued his attack, raking the Lancaster with long bursts of fire. By now, the mid-upper gunner, Flt Sgt B. Leach also picked up the fighter at 400 yards but could not get a bead on it until it broke away to port. Leach also scored hits on the Me410 as the fighter rolled off the top of its turn and dived away vertically.

The attack had taken its toll on the Lancaster, with the tailplane and rudder damaged and the port inner engine in flames, although the fire came under control

OC 635 Squadron, Wg Cdr S. 'Tubby' Baker DSO, DFC and Bar, pictured after he had completed his 100th operation for 8 Group. (via Author)

when the engine was feathered. The starboard inner also had to feathered and the starboard fuel was holed. Swales ordered his crew to don their parachutes but rescinded the order when he realised that PB538 continued to perform as normal and even dared to climb. The main concern was how long the electrics would last because the generator was driven off the inner engines and, without current, the crucial DR compass would fail. Approaching a cold front, the loss of blind-flying instruments put the aircraft in perilous danger and, once again, the captain ordered his crew to don parachutes and bail out. Once the last one was safely away from the Lancaster, Swales attempted to make a crash landing but, as he approached the ground, PB538 struck some H/T cables and spun into the ground at La Chappelle-aux-Bois, south of Valenciennes. For his actions that day, Capt E. Swales was awarded Bomber Command's last and 8 Group's third VC of the Second World War. Part of his citation, which was gazetted on 24 April 1945 read, 'Intrepid in attack, courageous in the face of danger, he did his duty to the last, giving his life that his comrades might live.'

March 1945 – The Allies push into Germany

The US 1st and 3rd Armies had been positioned on the western bank of the Rhine since late February and were poised to secure a bridgehead at Remagen, south of Bonn. The opposing German forces were concentrated in Cologne, in direct opposition to the US 1st Army and, once again, Bomber Command was called in to soften them up. In broad daylight, on 2 March, 858 bombers set out in two waves to bomb the city, the first wave being led by 8 Group's *Oboe* Mosquitoes who dropped *Wanganui* Smoke Puffs on a target free of cloud. The result was total destruction of what remained of the city and the cratering was so severe, that several hundred armoured vehicles were trapped, only to be picked off by Tactical Air Force attacks later in the day. Four days after, the city was captured by US forces, making this the last of 31 raids on Cologne which began in May 1940.

Another city that was to be visited by the RAF for the last time was the long-suffering Essen. A total of 1,079 aircraft, the most ever sent to this target, were despatched on 11 March, once again in daylight. The target was completely cloud-covered but the *Oboe* Mosquito sky-markers were accurately placed and 4,661 tons of bombs paralysed Essen until the arrival of American troops. The RAF had been bombing Essen since August 1940 and it is known that at least 7,000 of the population had been killed.

In contrast, Hildesheim suffered only one major Bomber Command raid for the entire war which destroyed 70% of the town on 22 March. Some 227 Lancasters

*A 4,000 lb 'Cookie' is manoeuvred into position towards Mosquito VI PF432 of
128 Squadron at Wyton before an attack on Berlin on 21 March 1945.
Having already served with 692 Squadron, PF432 was transferred to 180
and then 69 Squadron, before being SOC at Walm on 5 August 1947.
(via Author)*

and eight Mosquitoes from 1 and 8 Groups were detailed to attack the town's
railway yards but by the time the attack was over, 263 acres of Hildesheim had
been devastated. Four Lancasters were lost on this raid, none of them were from
8 Group who saw a rapid decline in 'heavy' losses on operations over Germany.

Following the success of the earlier attack on Cologne by Bomber Command,
Eisenhower planned on creating a second bridgehead to the north of the Ruhr.

The Lancasters of 156 Squadron are illuminated by TIs at 12,000 ft over Hanau on 18 March 1945. (www.ww2images.com)

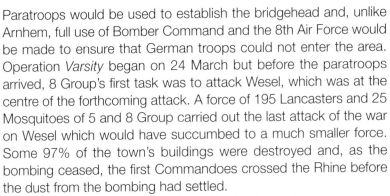

Paratroops would be used to establish the bridgehead and, unlike Arnhem, full use of Bomber Command and the 8th Air Force would be made to ensure that German troops could not enter the area. Operation *Varsity* began on 24 March but before the paratroops arrived, 8 Group's first task was to attack Wesel, which was at the centre of the forthcoming attack. A force of 195 Lancasters and 25 Mosquitoes of 5 and 8 Group carried out the last attack of the war on Wesel which would have succumbed to a much smaller force. Some 97% of the town's buildings were destroyed and, as the bombing ceased, the first Commandoes crossed the Rhine before the dust from the bombing had settled.

On 24 March, 8 Group's first attack of the day was on the marshalling yards at Sterkrade, 60 miles behind the German lines. The attack, involving 177 aircraft, 155 of which were Halifaxes, was led by 7 Squadron's CO Wg Cdr D. A. Cracknell, who map-read his way direct to the target which was skilfully marked by six *Oboe* Mosquitoes. The marshalling yard was soon obscured by smoke but under Cracknell's directions, the target was left in complete chaos. Gladbeck was also hit on 24 March, a town located on the northern edge of the Ruhr, very close to the new battle area. Sixteen PFF Lancasters and eight PFF Mosquitoes led 153 Halifaxes to carry out a devastating attack. The following day, 8 Group continued to lead attacks against towns on the main reinforcement routes to the new second front. Hannover, Münster and Osnabrück were all extensively bombed and, by the end of the day, Bomber Command had carried out 606 sorties in support of *Varsity* with the loss of just four aircraft, none of which were from 8 Group.

April/May 1945 – 'Eagles Nest', *Exodus*, *Manna* and victory!

By 1 April, the US 1st and 9th Armies joined up in the Soest region, completely surrounding the Ruhr armies. Both armies then made a parallel push across Germany towards Leipzig and Magdeburg, as the 2nd British Army headed for Bremen and Hamburg. While the US 1st Army was pushing forward, 8 Group led the first of two attacks on what was thought to be a large military barracks at Nordhausen. The first attack, by 247 Lancasters and eight Mosquitoes, in daylight on 3 April was very accurate but this did not stop another 243 Lancasters and nine Mosquitoes from attacking it again the following day as well. The 'barracks' was actually occupied by a large number of concentration-camp prisoners and foreign workers. These people were housed in a complex of underground tunnels for secret projects which had moved to Nordhausen after Bomber Command's attacks on Peenemünde.

Oil targets were hit hard on the night of 4/5 April, with raids on Leuna, Harburg and Lützkendorf by a total of 940 aircraft. The railway centres at Englesdorf and Mockau were attacked ahead of US troops on 10 April and the next day *Oboe* Mosquitoes pin-pointed their TIs on the marshalling yards at Bayreuth. The same day, fourteen PFF Lancasters marked the marshalling yards at Nuremberg accurately and without loss on either raid.

The last major raid of the Second World War by a major Bomber Command force against a German city took place on 14/15 April. The target was Potsdam and it was also the first time since March 1944 that a four-engined bomber had entered the Berlin defensive zone. The exact target within the city was the local barracks and railway yards but it is known that some bombs fell in the northern and eastern districts of Berlin as well. The raid was reasonably successful but up to 5,000 civilians were killed because they were so used to seeing Berlin being bombed heavily that they never thought it would happen to Potsdam. The route to the target was now virtually in Allied hands and, as a result, out of the force of 500 Lancasters and twelve Mosquitoes only two 'heavies' were shot down. One of these was 35 Squadron Lancaster III PB377, being flown by Fg Off V. B. Bowen-Norris. Whilst near the target, an engine caught fire and Bowen-Norris ordered his crew to bail out. After six of them had left and as he prepared to take to his own parachute, Bowen-Norris regained control and managed to reach Holland before he was finally forced to bail out safely. Of the six who bailed out near Potsdam, one was killed, one evaded capture and four spent the final days of the war behind wire.

On 16/17 April, the railway yards at Schwandorf were the target, with 167 Lancasters and eight Mosquitoes of 6 and 8 Groups taking part. Very accurate *Oboe* red TIs were skilfully backed up by tightly-packed greens and the resulting bombing matched the marking. The operation was marred by the loss of 8 Group's last Lancaster of the war after it collided with a 171 Squadron Halifax on a Bomber Support operation. Lancaster III PB403 of 156 Squadron, flown by Fg Off J. Jamieson and crew, struck the Halifax near Mürlenbach and both aircraft crashed into a wood called Kahle Köpfchen. Neither crew survived.

The naval base, airfield and town on the fortified island of Heligoland were attacked by 969 aircraft from all groups on 18 April. The PFF marked three A/Ps and from the *Oboe* TIs through to the final backers-up, the standard was high. Post-attack photography shows the island to be like a moonscape because of the amount of craters but this did not stop 9 and 617 Squadron from 5 Group dropping 36 *Tallboys* the following day.

Kiel was attacked by 107 Mosquitoes on 21/22 April, a raid that was described by the local diarist as '… it is no longer possible to spot which damage is new.' For 8 Group, the night saw its last losses of the Second World War with two Mosquitoes failing to return. Both were presumed to have crashed in the target area but how this came about is not known. First was 163 Squadron Mosquito XXV KB529 flown by Flt Lt W. G. Baker and Fg Off A. A. Hawthorne RCAF and secondly, 608 Squadron Mosquito XVI RV359 flown by Sqn Ldr E. S. Few DFC, AFC and Plt Off S. S. Campbell. Only Flt Lt Baker survived.

Harping back to the days of *Nickel* drops, 8 Group were asked to carry out a leaflet raid with a difference on 24/25 April, when 30 Mosquitoes and seven Lancasters dropped leaflets on eight POW camps where the British inmates were close to being liberated. The leaflets warned the Germans of the consequences for them if any harm came to the POWs. Medical supplies were also dropped at the Neubrandenburg camp north of Berlin.

No. 8 Group's final blow of the war came on 25 April with two large operations, one against the coastal batteries on Wangerooge and the other to Hitler's 'Eagle's Nest' at Berchtesgaden. The latter was led by MB Wg Cdr J. W. Fordham and his Deputy Flt Lt C. G. Hitchcock. Once the force of 359 Lancasters and sixteen Mosquitoes of 1, 5 and 8 Groups arrived over the target, they found the A/P easily in the clear mountain air. However, at least one of the mountains blocked the *Oboe* ground station's signal despite at least one Mosquito circling high above at 39,000 ft. The situation was overcome by Flt Lt Hitchcock who marked the target with his TIs, giving the Main Force the opportunity to make every bomb count on this morale-boosting target. All were hoping that Hitler was at home but, alas, unknown to the crews, he was already holed up in his bunker in Berlin, destined to take his own life eight days later.

This was the last PFF 'heavy' raid of the war, although the Mosquitoes would carry out one more raid on Kiel on 2/3 May. The PFF 'heavies' now found themselves employed in a completely different role, beginning with Operation *Exodus* on 26 April. Up to 7 May, 469 flights were made by Lancasters from 1, 5, 6 and 8 Groups to collect British POWs recently liberated from their camps. By the end of the operation, 75,000 men were flown back to England without incident. The PFF alone ferried 2,858 of them, the first being flown back by 8 Group's C-in-C, AVM D. Bennett.

Another non-combatant role that 8 Group took part in was Operation *Manna*, which began on 29 April. A large area of western Holland, which was still under

Approximately 10,000 cookies were dropped on the enemy by 8 Group's LNSF. This is the crew and ground crew of a 608 Squadron Mosquito at Downham Market, preparing to drop their last bombs on Kiel on 2/3 May 1945. Note the 635 Squadron codes 'F2-D' on the bomb trolley; this Lancaster's war is already over. (via Author)

German occupation, was approaching starvation and many had already died. The local German commander agreed a truce and Lancasters from 1, 3 and 8 Groups began dropping food supplies to the civilian population. PFF Mosquitoes marked each dropping zone and despite the stand of The Hague racecourse being burnt

down by an *Oboe* TI, the operation went well. Before 7 May, 2,835 Lancaster and 124 Mosquito flights were made during Operation *Manna* which delivered 6,672 tons of food parcels.

8 Group's swan song

On VE Day, 8 Group still had fifteen operational squadrons on strength, 109 Squadron having disbanded at Little Staughton on 30 April. As with the other Bomber Command groups, peace-time brought rapid changes as Commonwealth servicemen were given priority to return home and general strength began to shrink. Those crews remaining found themselves flying Cook's tours over bomb-damaged Germany and later the group was heavily involved in Operation *Dodge*, the repatriation of soldiers from the 8th Army and further afield.

On 21 May, 1945, AVM Don Bennett, the only Group Commander to serve a full term resigned his commission in order to stand for Parliament. He was replaced by AVM J. R. Whitley, who was transferred from his role as AOC 4 Group.

From June 1945 onwards, 8 Group began to reduce in size with 405 Squadron being the first post-war departure when it returned to Canada on 16 June. The same month saw 162 Squadron transferred to Transport Command asked with operating an Air Delivery Letter Service to Germany, Denmark, Norway and Italy. August saw the disbandment of 163 and 608 Squadrons and in September, 142, 156, 571, 582, 635 and 692 Squadrons were all dissolved. No.128 Squadron followed in October when it was transferred to 2 Group and moved to Moelsbroek in Belgium, to serve with 139 Wing and 1409 Flight was transferred to 47 Group.

When the hammer finally fell on 8 Group on 15 December 1945, only four squadrons were left to disperse amongst an air force that was only a shadow of its former self. Both 7 and 35 Squadrons went on to convert to the Lincoln; 105 Squadron was disbanded in February 1946; while 139 Squadron continued to fly the Mosquito until 1953, when it converted to Canberra.

'A' Flight NTU (Night Training Unit) (PFF) line up for their first 'peace-time' photograph at Warboys on 5 June 1945. (www.ww2images.com)

They also served. This is the Instrument Section of both 35 and 692 Squadrons enjoying the more relaxed atmosphere of peacetime operations at Graveley in July 1945. (www.ww2images.com)

Appendix

I

8 (Pathfinder Force) Group Statistics August 1942 to May 1945

Group Statistics

During its three-year existence the Pathfinder Force operated five types of aircraft: the Wellington, Stirling, Halifax, Lancaster and Mosquito. By early 1944 Don Bennett had finally achieved his aim of making 8 Group an all-Lancaster and Mosquito force and, as a result, the high sortie rates of these types are reflected in the following statistics.

Only 156 Squadron brought the Wellington to 8 Group in August 1942 and flew just 305 sorties. However, seventeen aircraft were lost which equated to 5.6%, the highest loss statistic achieved by a single type in 8 Group.

The Stirling was introduced by 7 Squadron in August 1940 and was destined to operate the type until August 1943. It was the only unit in 8 Group to fly the Stirling, carrying out 826 sorties and losing 37 aircraft, 4.5%, in the process.

The Halifax was flown by one of the founding units, 35 Squadron until March 1944. Only 405 Squadron also flew the type but they only joined 8 Group in April 1943 and by September their Halifaxes had been replaced. Therefore the bulk of the 2,106 Halifax sorties were flown by 35 Squadron and 77 were lost, resulting in a loss rate of 3.7%.

The Lancaster featured prominently from the start within 8 Group, serving with 7, 35, 83, 97, 156, 405, 582 and 635 Squadrons to the end of the Second World War.

As a result, the bomber flew 19,601 sorties for 8 Group but at a cost of 444 aircraft which, when viewed by a loss ratio of 2.3%, appeared to be an acceptable figure in the eyes of the senior staff of Bomber Command.

The statistical prizes go to the Mosquito which served with 105, 109, 128, 139, 142, 162, 163, 571, 582, 608, 627 and 692 Squadrons and 1409 Flight. The Mosquitoes of 8 Group had performed exceptionally well and, since its formation, they had flown 28,215 sorties, with the loss of just 100 aircraft (0.4%), 70 of them lost by 139 Squadron alone. Approximately 26,000 tons of bombs, of which nearly 10,000 of them were cookies, were dropped on Germany.

Worthy of special note is 1409 Flight which carried out 1,364 valuable PAMPA operations on 632 occasions, with the loss of just three aircraft (0.2%) since its formation at Oakington on 1 April 1943.

Total sorties for 8 Group totalled 51,053 with 675 aircraft lost (2.3%)

Appendix

II

Aircraft Types

Vickers Wellington III

The Wellington, more affectionately known as the 'Wimpy', was designed by Barnes Wallis, whose well-proven geodetic design made the twin-engined bomber an aircraft that could take a lot of punishment. The Wellington had a remarkable career which began in October 1938 and continued, albeit in trainer form, until 1953.

Within 8 Group, only the Wellington III had a part to play, with founding unit 156 Squadron, who had been operating the type from its formation in February 1942. From January 1943, the unit began to receive the Lancaster and by the autumn, the Wellington, which had been the mainstay of Bomber Command, was removed from front line operations in the European theatre.

Power: Two 1,500 hp Bristol Hercules XI engines
Span: 86 ft 2 in
Length: 64 ft 7 in
Performance: Max speed 255 mph; climb rate 930ft/min; ceiling 18,996 ft
Armament: Two .303 in in nose, four .303 in rear turret and a pair of .303 in in beam positions. Up to 4,500 lbs of bombs.
Crew: 6

Short Stirling I & III

The Stirling was the RAF's first four-engined bomber and first entered service with Pathfinder finding founding member, 7 Squadron, at Leeming in August 1940. Unfairly criticized by post-war historians, the Stirling was an excellent aircraft, which was popular with its crews despite the aircraft's infamous Achilles heel; lack of altitude. This came about because of the original 'misinformed' specification stating that the aircraft should have a

wingspan of less than 100 ft in order to fit into the 'standard' RAF hangar of the day!

No.7 Squadron was the only unit to operate the Stirling I and III in 8 Group and this did not come to an end until August 1943, following conversion to the Lancaster.

Power: (III) Four 1,650 hp Bristol Hercules XVI engines
Span: 99 ft 1 in
Length: 87 ft 3 in
Performance: Max speed 270 mph at 14,500 ft; range 2,010 miles with 3,500 lb of bombs, 590 miles with 14,000 lb of bombs; ceiling 17,500 ft
Armament: Two .303 in in nose and dorsal turrets, four .303 in rear turret. Up to 14,000 lbs of bombs.
Crew: 7–8

Handley Page Halifax II & III

While only two 8 Group units, 35 and 405 Squadron, operated the Halifax in Mk II and Mk III, the Handley-Page built bomber was widely used by Bomber Command.

First flown in October 1939, the Halifax entered service with 35 Squadron at Leeming in November 1940 and was destined to remain at the forefront of Bomber Command operations until the end of the war. Although overshadowed by the statistics achieved by the Lancaster, the Halifax still managed to carry out 83,072 sorties for Bomber Command and drop 227,610 tons of bombs.

By September 1943, the Halifax I & II were used for less hazardous duties but, with the arrival of the better performing Mk III, the bomber was back in the front line over Europe again from February 1944. By the summer, 26 Halifax squadrons were operating over Europe, although by then the Pathfinders, 35 and 405 Squadrons had converted to the Lancaster.

Power: (II) Four 1,280 hp Rolls-Royce Merlin XX engines. (III) Four 1,650 hp Bristol Hercules XVI engines.
Span: 104 ft 2 in
Length: 71 ft 7 in
Performance: (III) Max Speed 282mph at 13,500 ft; range 1,030 miles with 8,000 lb of bombs; ceiling 18,600 ft with an 8,000 lb load
Armament: (III) Single Vickers K in nose, four .303in in dorsal and rear turret. Up to 14,000 lbs of bombs.
Crew: 7

Avro Lancaster I, III & VI

Quite possibly the most famous and certainly the most successful bomber of the Second World War, the Avro Lancaster was the shot in the arm that Bomber Command so desperately needed. It was Don Bennett's goal from the outset to equip all of 8 Group's 'heavy' squadrons with the Lancaster; a task that he managed to achieve in early 1944.

First flown in January 1941, the Lancaster entered service with 44 Squadron at Waddington just eleven months later. The bomber quickly made its mark on Bomber Command and, by July 1943, only one Lancaster was being lost on operations for 132 tons of bombs dropped. Compare this to the Halifax, with one aircraft lost for 56 tons of bombs and the Stirling, trailing in with 41 tons dropped for every aircraft lost.

Power: (I) Four 1,640 hp Rolls-Royce Merlin 20 or 22 engines, (III) 1,640 hp Merlin or (VI) Merlin 85.
Span: 102 ft
Length: 69 ft 6 in
Performance: Max speed 287mph at 11,500 ft; range 1,660 miles with 14,000 lb of bombs; ceiling 24,500 ft
Armament: Two .303 in in nose and dorsal turrets, four .303 in in the rear turret. Up to 14,000 lbs of bombs (Special variants could carry up to the 22,000 lb Grand Slam but these were not operated by 8 Group)
Crew: 7–8

de Havilland Mosquito IV, VI, IX, XVI, XX, XXV

The Mosquito is unsurpassed in being the most successful product of the British aircraft industry during the Second World War. Its versatility allowed the design to be used as a fighter, fighter-bomber, night-fighter and photographic–reconnaissance aircraft or as a pure bomber, where it performed without fault for Bomber Command from May 1942 to the end of the war and beyond.

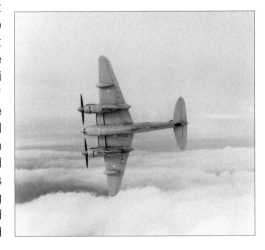

The Mosquito IV was the most prolific variant operated by 8 Group up to late 1944, by which time, Bennett had gained enough aircraft for the LNSF, which kept the pressure on Nazi Germany even while the 'heavies' rested. Berlin was a specialty for the LNSF which visited the German capital on 170 separate occasions. From February 20/21, the LNSF attacked Berlin on 36 consecutive nights! Loss rates were incredibly low, averaging one aircraft per 2,000 sorties carried out; a comfortable Bomber Command record for the Mosquito. Their speed, which was at first 100 mph faster than the Lancaster, allowed the Mosquitoes time to take off after the main force but still arrive ahead of them to mark the target and then be home again long before any four-engined type had crossed the Dutch border!

Power: (IV) Two 1,250 hp Rolls-Royce Merlin 21, (XVI) two 1,680 hp Merlin 72 or 73 or two Merlin 76 or 77.
Span: 54 ft 2 in
Length: 40 ft 9½ in
Performance: (IV) Max Speed 380 mph at 17,000 ft, (XVI) 415 mph at 28,000 ft; (IV) range 2,040 miles, (XIV) 1,370 miles with a 4,000 lb bomb load; (IV) ceiling 28,800 ft.
Armament: (IV) 2,000 lb bomb load, (XVI) 4,000 lb bomb load
Crew: 2

German night-fighters

A total of 7,953 aircraft from Bomber Command were lost during night operations in the Second World War; 5,833 of these were shot down by Luftwaffe night-fighters. As the war progressed, the Nachtjägd (German night-fighter) became more organised and from 1943 onwards posed the greatest threat to Allied aircrew over occupied Europe and in some cases over Britain as well.

Messerschmitt Bf 110

By far the most common of all of the Luftwaffe night-fighters was an aircraft that first flew in May 1936. The Messerschmitt Bf 110 was a versatile aircraft that may have proved inadequate in daylight during the early years of the war, but would prove to be a lethal and efficient killing machine at night.

As early as July 1940, Herman Göring called for a new Nachtjagdgeschwader (night-fighter squadron) of which I/NJG 1 became the first with the Bf 110C-2. At this stage, crews relied heavily upon radar-assisted searchlights to expose their prey but it was not long before the aircraft were being more accurately plotted to their target by Würzburg FuMG 62 ground radar.

By 1941, it was clear that the fighter needed its own radar and using Bf 110E-1/U1s, I/NJG 1 successfully tested the Telefunken FuG 202 (Lichtenstein BC) AI (Airborne Interception) radar. By July 1942, the more powerful FuG 212 Lichtenstein was arriving on front line units in the Bf 110F-4. Powered by a pair of Daimler-Benz DB 601F-1 engines and armed with four 7.92mm MG 17 machine guns and a pair of Mauser MG 151/20 cannons, the F-4 was the first pure night-fighter of the Bf 110 family. Many famous German night-fighter aces such as Becker, Falk, Lent, Meurer,

Schnaufer (121 nocturnal kills flying the Bf 110) and Strieb achieved high victory tallies with the fighter.

The attacking technique for a Bf 110 crew was usually to approach the bomber from behind and below and then, at the crucial moment, pitch the fighter to 50° and rake the unsuspecting aircraft from front to back. This technique was made even easier with the introduction of a pair of 20mm MG-FF/M cannon installed behind the cockpit and positioned at an angle of between 60° and 70°. The weapon's fit was named schräge Musik (jazz), and proved to be a highly effective form of attack.

By late 1943, the Bf 110 was not expected to still be in service, being superseded by the Messerschmitt Me 210. However, the Me 210 did not prove to be up to the job and the Bf 110 was developed still further to the final and most successful 'G' series. The Bf 110G-4 introduced the FuG 202 radar and by mid-1944 had equipped the majority of Luftwaffe night-fighter units which covered the skies from Denmark to the Romanian border.

Despite a critical beginning in the daylight role, the Bf 110 night-fighter was definitely one of the most efficient all-purpose aircraft of the Second World War.

Power: (G-4) Two Daimler-Benz 605B-1 engines
Span: 53 ft 4¾ in
Length: 41 ft 6¾ in
Performance: Max speed (C-4) 349 mph at 22,965 ft; climb rate 2,165 ft/min; ceiling 32,810 ft
Armament: Four 7.9mm MG 17 and two MG 151 cannons; schräge Musik two 20mm MG-FF/M cannons.
Crew: 2

Junkers Ju 88

The largest of all of the Luftwaffe night-fighters, by some margin, was the Junkers Ju 88 which was originally designed as a four-seat bomber, first flying, like the Bf 110, in 1936. The Ju 88 was a very successful design from the outset and the first of two significant night-fighter variants was introduced in 1940, with the Ju 88C-2. The 3,200 C-series aircraft were built for the night-fighter role, the V-6b and C-6c, introducing the Lichtenstein BC and Lichtenstein C-1 radars. Sensors that could home onto the RAF's *Monica*, such as the FuG 227 Flensburg radar, and the FuG 350 Naxos which picked up H2S signals were also carried by Ju 88s. This, combined with a schräge Musik fit, made the Ju 88 a lethal opponent.

The hard working C-series was replaced by the Ju 88G-series from mid-1943, an aircraft that was refined into another lethal foe for the RAF Bomber Command crews. The last major night-variant had a half-sized ventral pack containing up to four 20 mm MG cannon, plus a pair of upward firing MG 151s. The fighter's long endurance, superb performance and healthy collection of electronic devices wreaked havoc amongst the bomber streams and the only blessing for RAF crews was that the Ju 88G was not introduced earlier in the war.

Power: (G-1) Two 1,700 hp BMW 801D-2 engines
Span: 65 ft 7½ in
Length: (excluding radar) 47 ft 8½ in
Performance: Max Speed 356 mph; ceiling 29,000 ft
Armament: Four 20 mm MG 151 firing forward and two MG 151 cannons firing upwards.
Crew: 4

Messerschmitt Bf 109G

Despite not being a dedicated night-fighter, the ubiquitous Bf 109 was undoubtedly encountered by many RAF aircrew. The most likely candidate was the Bf 109G which was introduced from 1942 with an uprated DB 605 engine, increased armament and the ability to fire rockets.

Bf 109 attacks were increasingly reported as the war came to an end, as more of 8 Groups were being flown in daylight.

Power: (G-2) One 1,475 hp Daimler-Benz 605A-1 engine
Span: 32 ft 6½ in
Length: 29 ft
Performance: Max Speed 406 mph at 28,540 ft; ceiling 39,370 ft
Armament: Two 7.9 mm MG 17 machine guns and one 20 mm MG 151/20 cannon; provision for rockets.
Crew: 1

Focke Wulf Fw 190A series

By mid 1943, the formidable Fw 190 was being diverted from daylight duties against the USAAF 8th Air Force to the growing night-time activities of RAF Bomber Command. The Luftwaffe's night-fighter wings were keen to adopt a smaller, faster fighter specifically to deal with the increasing number of Mosquitoes which were easily outpacing their twin-engine counterparts. NJG 1 and 3 operated a small number of Fw 190s alongside their Bf 110s and Ju 88s but it was clear that the Luftwaffe needed to employ the fighter with a new strategy.

The new technique, which began in the spring of 1943, was called Wilde Sau (Wild Boar) and, rather than being guided to the target by a ground station, the pilot, after being guided to the general area of the bomber stream, used his own judgement as to when to attack. Fw 190 pilots were given free rein to find bombers which were often highlighted by the ground fires that they had created. Although Wilde Sau was only a short-term solution pending more advanced equipment, the technique was employed by the Fw 190 until May 1944.

Other dedicated Fw 190 night-fighter units were created during this period, including JG 300, 301 and 302, all of whom at first had to scrounge aircraft away from day units. Wilde Sau units eventually began to receive their own aircraft which were modified with exhaust dampers, blind-flying equipment and the Fw190A-4/R-11 through to the A-8/R11s which were fitted with FuG 217 or FuG radar equipment.

Power: (A-3) One 1,700 hp BMW 801 D-2 engine
Span: 34 ft 5½ in
Length: 28 ft 10½ in

Performance: Max Speed 382 mph at 19,685 ft; ceiling 34,775 ft
Armament: (A-8) Four 20mm MG 151/20E cannons, two 13mm MG 131 machine-guns.
Crew: 1

Heinkel He 219A-5

The only aircraft listed here that was actually designed from the outset for night-fighter operations should have been the most successful Axis aircraft of the Second World War. One of the most sophisticated aircraft designed during the war, the He 219 Uhu (Eagle Owl) was not only fitted with the most advanced radar systems ever conceived, it was also equipped with ejection seats.

Luckily for the British bomber crews, the development of the Uhu was a rocky road and only 294 were ever built, making an encounter very rare.

Power: Two 1,800 hp Daimler-Benz DB 603E V-12 engines
Span: 60 ft 8 in
Length: 51 ft
Performance: Max Speed 385 mph; ceiling 30,500 ft
Armament: Four 20mm MG 151 cannons under fuselage, two 20mm MG 151 cannon in the wing roots and a pair of 30mm MK 108 schräge Musik cannons behind cockpit.
Crew: 2

Messerschmitt Me 410

A development of the Me 210, which was earmarked to replace the Bf 110 in the night-fighter role, the Me 410 was a moderately successful fighter-bomber and night-fighter. However, in night skies, the aircraft was a rarity and would more likely be found intruding over Britain. The twin-engine fighter was encountered on several occasions by RAF bomber crews.

Power: Two 1,726 hp Daimler-Benz DB 603A V-12 engines
Span: 53 ft 7 in
Length: 41 ft 2 in
Performance: Max speed 388 mph; ceiling 32,800 ft
Armament: Two 7.92 mm MG 17 machine guns, two 20 mm MG 151/20 cannons and two 13 mm MG 131 machine guns.
Crew: 2

Dornier Do 217J-1 & N

Developed by the Dornier Do 17, the 217 had the general appearance of its older sibling but incorporated a new structure and aerodynamic design. The result was a very efficient and versatile machine that was produced in large numbers as a bomber, torpedo-carrier, reconnaissance aircraft and, ultimately, a night-fighter.

The first night-fighter variant, the Do 217J, first appeared in 1941 with a solid nose for a bank of four machine guns and four cannons, plus an area to house the radar antennae. Simultaneously, the Do 217N appeared which, unlike the J, had BMW radials, the N had more aerodynamic Daimler-Benz engines. Some 364 of the 1,925 Do 217s built were converted into night-fighters which were never as popular with the Luftwaffe crews as the Ju88 and the Bf110. Regardless, they remained in service until early 1944, being particularly effective when using the upward firing schräge Musik.

Power: (N-2) Two 1,750 hp Daimler-Benz DB 603A engines
Span: 62 ft 4 in
Length: 62 ft
Performance: Max speed 320 mph at 19,685 ft; ceiling 29,200 ft
Armament: Four 7.92 mm MG 17 machine-guns in solid nose and four 20 mm MG 151/20 cannon, plus four 20 mm MG 151/20 in schräge Musik position.
Crew: 4

German Flak Guns

The entire anti-aircraft defence of Germany was placed in the hands of the Luftwaffe in 1935 and this continued until the end of the Second World War. On the outbreak of war, 6,700 2 cm and 3.7 cm flaks and a further 2,628 heavy guns were already in place in Germany, more than double the amount deployed in Britain. The heavy guns were made up of the 10.5 cm Flak 38 and 39 while the bulk was the hugely successful 8.8 cm Flak 18, 36 and 37. By mid 1944, the latter had increased to 11,000 alone, which included a large number 12.8 cm Flak 40 guns.

The 8.8 cm Flak was by far the most effective anti-aircraft weapon of the Second World War and prolific too, with 21,310 of them built. The weapon could fire between 15 and 20 rounds per minute and had an effective range of around 25,000 ft but, with a muzzle velocity of 2,690 ft per second, could reach up to 39,000 ft, leaving no place for any Allied bomber to hide.

A total of 675 Pathfinder bombers are believed to have been shot down directly or through enemy flak.

Appendix

III

The Pathfinder crews' eight duties

Each and every Pathfinder crew was expected to carry out eight specific duties although, from an official point of view, these were actually applied to the aircraft. Some crews proved to be more adept at carrying out a particular task and, in such a case, they would be selected for this duty.

The eight duties were:
1 'Rookie' PFF crews were always given the role of 'Supporter' within the first main group of the marker force. This was simply to increase the number of bombers over the target during the first wave of the attack.
2 Ahead of the main force were the 'Windowers' who dropped *Window* to disrupt the enemy's radar.
3 Tasked with estimating the mean point of impact (MPI), the 'Backers-up' later called 'Visual Centerers' dropped their TIs on this point.
4 Turning points were highlighted by the 'Route Markers' with TIs to help the main force reach the target.
5 Using *H2S*, the 'Blind Illuminators' dropped flares blind to aid the 'Visual Markers' and during *Newhaven* raids.
6 Only the cream of the PFF were selected as 'Primary Visual Markers'.
7 *H2S* or *Oboe* was used by the 'Blind Markers' for dropping TIs and sky markers.
8 Marking blindly using *H2S*, the 'Recenterers' usually arrived over the target half way through a raid to re-mark in an effort to prevent any bombing from undershooting or creeping back.

Appendix

IV

8 Group Squadrons August 1942 to August 1945

7 Squadron   'MG' Transferred from 3 Group in August '42.

Aircraft   Stirling I from August '40; Stirling III arrived March '43, operated until August '43; Lancaster I & III arrived from May '43.

Stations   Oakington 29 October '40, to Mepal 25 July '45.

35 Squadron   'TL' Transferred from 4 Group August '42.

Aircraft   Halifax II from October '41 to January '44; Halifax III from October '43 to March '44. Lancaster I & III from March '44 to September '49.

Stations   Graveley 15 August '42, to Stradishall 18 September '46.

83 Squadron   'OL' Transferred from 5 Group August '42. To 5 Group control from 18 April '44 onwards.

Aircraft   Lancaster I & III from May '42 to July '46.

Stations   Wyton 15 August '42, to Coningsby 18 April '44.

97 Squadron   'OF' Transferred from 5 Group April '43. Returned to 5 Group control until the end of the war from 18 April '44.

Aircraft   Lancaster I & III from January '42.

Stations   Bourn 18 April '43, dets Graveley, Gransden Lodge & Oakington; to Coningsby 18 April '44.

105 Squadron   'GB' Transferred from 2 Group 1 June '43.

Aircraft   Mosquito IV from November '41 to March '44; Mosquito IX from June '43 to August '45; Mosquito XVI from March '44 to February '46.

Stations   Marham 22 September '42 to 23 March '44, Bourn to 29 June '45, Upwood to 1 February '46 – DB.

109 Squadron   'HS' Transferred from WIDU August '42.

Aircraft   Lancaster I from July '42 to October '42; Mosquito IV from December '42 to May '44; Mosquito IX from June '43 to September '45; Mosquito XVI from March '44 to September '45.

Stations   Wyton 7 August '42, to Marham 5 July '43, to Little Staughton 2 April '44 to 30 April '45 - DB.

128 Squadron   'M5' RF at Wyton September '44

Aircraft   Mosquito XX from September '44 to November '44; Mosquito XXV from October '44 to November '44; Mosquito XVI from Oct 44 to Mar 46.

Stations   Wyton 15 September '44, to Warboys 22 June '45.

139 Squadron   'XD' Transferred from 2 Group June '43.

Aircraft   Mosquito IV from June '42 to July '44; Mosquito IX from September '43 to August '44; Mosquito XX from December

'43 to August '45; Mosquito XVI from February '44 to July '48; Mosquito XXV from October '44 to May '45.

Stations   Marham 29 September '42, to Wyton 4 July '43, to Upwood 1 February '44, to Hemswell 4 February '46.

142 Squadron   '4H' RF at Gransden Lodge October '44. DB 28 September '45.

Aircraft   Mosquito XXV from October '44 to September '45.

Stations   Gransden Lodge 25 October '44.

156 Squadron   'GT' Transferred from 1 Group August '42. DB 25 September '45.

Aircraft   Wellington III from February '42 to January '43; Lancaster I & III from January '43 to September '45.

Stations   Warboys 8 August '42, to Upwood 5 March '44, to Wyton 27 June '45.

162 Squadron   'CR' RF at Bourn December '44. DB 14 July '46.

Aircraft   Mosquito XXV from December '44 to July '46; Mosquito XX February '45 to July '46.

Stations   Bourn 16 December '44, to Blackbushe 10 July '45.

163 Squadron   RF at Wyton January '45. DB 10 August '45.

Aircraft   Mosquito XXV January '45 to May '45; Mosquito XVI May '45 to Aug '45.

Stations   Wyton 25 January '45.

405 Squadron   'LQ' Transferred from 6 Group April '43. To Canada June '45.

Aircraft	Halifax II from April '42 to September '43; Lancaster I & III from August '43 to May '45; Lancaster X from May '45 to September '45.
Stations	Gransden Lodge 19 April '43, to Linton-on-Ouse 26 May '45.

571 Squadron '8K' Formed at Downham Market April '44. DB 20 September '45.

Aircraft	Mosquito XVI from April '44 to September '45.
Stations	Downham Market 5 April '44, det Graveley, to Oakington 24 April '44, to Warboys 20 July '45.

582 Squadron '60' Formed from 'C' Flts of 7 & 156 Squadrons at Little Staughton Apr '44. DB 10 September '45.

Aircraft	Lancaster I & III from April '44 to September '45.
Stations	Little Staughton 1 April '44.

608 Squadron '6T' Re-formed at Downham Market August '44. DB 24 August '45.

Aircraft	Mosquito XX from August '44 to April '45; Mosquito XXV from October '44 to April '45; Mosquito XVI from March '45 to August '45.
Stations	Downham Market 1 August '44.

627 Squadron 'A2' Formed at Oakington 12 November '43. Transferred to 5 Group at Woodhall Spa 15 April '44. DB and renumbered 109 Sqn.

Aircraft	Mosquito IV from 12 November '43 to 30 September '45; Mosquito XX from July '44 to September '45; Mosquito XXV from October '44 to September '45; Mosquito XVI from March '45 to September '45.
Stations	Oakington 12 November '43, to Woodhall Spa 15 April '44.

635 Squadron   'F2' Formed Downham Market March '44. DB 1 September '45.

    Aircraft   Lancaster III from March '44 to August '45; Lancaster VI from July '44 to November '44.

    Stations   Downham Market 20 March '44.

692 Squadron   'P3' Formed Graveley January '44. DB 20 September '45.

    Aircraft   Mosquito IV from January '44 to June '44; Mosquito XVI from March '44 to September '45.

    Stations   Graveley 1 January '44, to Gransden Lodge 4 June '45.

1409 Meteorological Flight   'AE' Formed at Oakington 1 April '43. To Lyneham and 47 Gp control with Liberators on 10 October '45.

    Aircraft   Mosquito IV, VI, IX, XV, XVI.

    Stations   Oakington 1 April '43, to Bourn November '43, to Wyton 8 January '44, to Upwood 5 July '45.

Appendix

V

Early Radar and Navigational Aids

GEE

The first significant radio navigational aid used by Bomber Command entered operational service from August 1942, although it had been experimented with twelve months earlier. Radio transmissions from three ground based positions emitted a precisely timed signal which was received via an oscilloscope positioned in the navigators position. The device in the aircraft was nicknamed the 'Goon Box' because it was so easy to use.

On receiving the transmission, the navigator could accurately plot the position of the aircraft to within a mile over Germany and approximately 165 yards when over Britain. The further away from the radio transmitters which were all based in Britain before 1944, the less accurate the device became. Its maximum effective range was 350 miles but beyond that the system still set the aircraft on a fairly accurate course to the target. The main shortcoming of the device was that the Germans did not take long to work out how to jam it and, in a very short space of time, its use beyond the Dutch coast was limited. However, its use for crews returning home was initially more appreciated than its ability to find the target. This factor alone compensated for any of its failings.

H2S

H2S was a10 cm radar fitted below the rear fuselage which transmitted a fan shaped beam. The beam was very broad in the vertical but narrow in the horizontal and rotated around the vertical axis to scan the ground below the aircraft. The signal from the radar bounced back to the aircraft from the ground and the time it took to return was proportional to the distance the ground was from the aircraft. A cathode ray tube (CRT) display would register the return as a dot relative to the position of the aircraft.

Depending on the type of terrain the aircraft was flying a different response would be received by the aircraft. When over water, the H2S beam was reflected away from the aircraft so nothing would appear on the CRT. However, when over land, a larger proportion of the emitted energy from the radar would bounce back and appear as dots on the CRT. When over a dense built up area, a larger amount of energy would return to the aircraft to display a higher proportion of dots. The return was not affected by the weather making dense cloud cover irrelevant.

Crews became very skilled at interpreting the picture that H2S presented them and its introduction from January 1943 in the Stirling and Halifax gave Bomber Command yet another advantage. H2S was not perfect though, although if a target was coastal, the lack of a return from water made ports in particular clearly stand out on the CRT. Rivers and lakes were also good points of reference and H2S was good for large built up targets such as factories.

Although H2S was used until the end of the Second World War, examples of the device inevitably fell into enemy hands and, to counter it, the Germans developed the FuG (*Funkgerät*) 350 Naxos radar detector. Fitted into enemy night-fighters, Naxos could home onto any bomber using its H2S.

OBOE

Oboe was the codename given to the ground-controlled blind bombing device which was incredibly accurate for the day. The device could operate at heights up to 30,000ft and speeds in excess of 300mph but could still achieve an operational error of just 300 yards; this distance reduced dramatically at lower altitudes.

Developed by 109 Squadron, it was initially trialled using a pair of pressurised Wellington VIs although it would be forever associated during the Second World War with the high-performance Mosquito.

The bombing device was controlled by two ground stations; one was codenamed 'Cat' and was based in Norfolk, the other, 'Mouse', was positioned in Kent. The two stations could accurately place an aircraft directly on track to the target and inform the aircraft when to drop its TIs, bombs or both. While *Oboe* was not expert in measuring direction, it could measure range with an accuracy that allowed the attacking aircraft to fly on a curved track at a constant distance from the ground station. This was achieved by signals transmitted from the ground station to the aircraft, which were then amplified and sent back to ground station. Using both 'Cat' and 'Mouse' the aircraft's distance was quickly worked out by plotting where both ground stations' signals intersected.

The sortie began at first with the aircraft starting the arced track over the North Sea and flying on a southerly heading towards the target. The pilot then flew the route keeping 'Cat' at a constant range, which was the same range to the target; effectively flying a circle around the Norfolk-based ground station. The pilot knew whether he was on track on or not by a tone in his earphones. If he was closer to 'Cat', he would receive dots and if he was further away, dashes were received; a continuous tone meant that the arc was being followed accurately.

As the aircraft closed on the target, 'Mouse', which was already recording the approach speed and height, started to emit warning signals. A signal would be sent when the aircraft was three minutes from the target, followed by a final signal which would inform the navigator to release the TIs onto the target. Once the navigator had pressed the bomb release, the aircraft's transmitter was instantly cut, at which point the two ground stations would know the exact time of release.

As with devices that rely on signals, there were some disadvantages, but these were few, purely because of the excellent performance of the Mosquito, which was the main aircraft to use *Oboe*. German night-fighter crews could home in on *Oboe*, but interceptions were rare and casualties even rarer.

MONICA

This was a warning device for the benefit of the rear gunner. The device worked by radiating signals from the rear of the bomber which were only reflected back when another aircraft was behind it. Each echo made a 'pip' sound into the intercom and as the enemy aircraft closed on the bomber the 'pips' sounded closer together.

The initial obvious disadvantage was that *Monica* did not distinguish between friend or foe nor did it give any indication of whether the enemy fighter was high, low, left or right! The former disadvantage turned *Monica* into more trouble than it was worth when bombers began flying in tightly packed formations or streams. The device would then continually pick up all of the friendly aircraft around it driving the crew mad with a continuous solid tone.

When the Luftwaffe began to introduce its version of AI radar, SN2, once again *Monica* proved more of a hindrance as the signals it was emitted were easily picked up by the enemy fighter which would home in on the bomber.

First used operationally on June 16/17, 1943, the device was later modified to Mk IIIA standard which entailed using a visual indicator rather than acoustic. The same disadvantages were still in place and the device was generally turned off.

FISHPOND

As the availability of H2S began to spread through Bomber Command, a new enemy warning device was introduced to supersede *Monica*. At first given the code name Mousetrap, the device had to be renamed Fishpond not long after as the former was already in use.

Fishpond used the same basic theory of reflecting echoes as *Monica* but received the returned information via CRT instead. Designed by the physicist and radio astronomer Sir Bernard Lovell (1913-2012), *Fishpond* made use of the H2S which up until then only displayed signals at the height the aircraft was flying. Fishpond, however, then exploited the base not used, that of the radiations between terra firma and the aircraft.

Making use of the H2S scanner, any echo from an enemy aircraft was projected onto a separate tube. On the display, the ground return around the edge looked like a halo while the centre looked like a black infinite black hole. All airborne objects between the ground and the aircraft were displayed on the tube in their exact position.

The advantages over *Monica* were that the 'pip' was replaced by a silent visual blip on the screen and the bearing and distance of the enemy aircraft could be worked out. Even if several blips were on the screen, any that were moving towards the bomber were most likely to be night-fighters. There was also the added advantage that mid-air collisions were reduced as the crews now knew where the rest of the bombers were.

The main disadvantage was that the device was geared to a fighter approaching from below which, at the time, especially when *schräge Musik* was introduced, was generally where the enemy would attack. The device was eventually rendered as useless as *Monica* when the Luftwaffe introduced *Naxos* which homed in on any signal emitted by either the H2S or *Fishpond*.

BOOZER

First used on November 13/14, 1942 by 7 Squadron Stirlings during an attack on Genoa, the device warned aircraft when ground defences were taking a particular interest in them. A red light came on in the Wireless Operator's compartment when searchlights or guns were vectoring the bomber. By receiving this early warning the pilot could take evasive action before being coned or shot up by predicted flak.

Fully introduced in early 1943, the rearward-looking aerial was fitted in the tail of the bomber. It was particularly good at giving crews notice of when their aircraft was being monitored by ground-based *Würzburg* radar, and by *FuG 202/212* transmissions from a night-fighter's AI radar.

Appendix

Pathfinder jargon buster

A/P	Aiming Point
API	The Air Position Indicator worked via a complex web of pipes and wires via the ASI, altimeter and DR compass. It was able to give the exact position of the aircraft in nil wind conditions. The indicator had the ability to compensate for any violent manoeuvre, changes in speed and/or height.
Boozer	(See Appendix V)
Bullseye	A long-range, cross-country flight usually carried by OTU crews in conjunction with ground defences. Objective was to give fledgling crews experience of what conditions would be like over the target. Pathfinder crews under training also dropped marker bombs and flares.
Blockbuster	A 4,000, 8,000 or 12,000 lb HC bomb.
Coned	When a bomber was held by more than one searchlight.
Cookie	A 4,000 lb bomb.
Cope	A successful *Oboe* sortie
DMB	Deputy Master Bomber
DR	Dead Reckoning

FIDO Fog Investigation Dispersal Operation. Burners positioned at intervals along the edge of a runway; the rising heat from which would help to disperse fog.

'fighter flares' Dropped by German aircraft to 'mark' the bomber routes into and away from the target.

Fishpond (See Appendix V)

GH A blind bombing radar device which worked like *Oboe* but in reverse.

GPI Group Position Indicator.

H2S (See Appendix V)

Heavie A four-engined bomber.

LNSF Light Night Striking Force. In early 1944, the LNSF was formed in 8 Group, initially with 139, 627 and 692 Squadrons, although 627 soon left to join 5 Group's marker force. Later, 128, 571 and 608 Squadrons joined the LNSF and participated in the force's frequent nocturnal roving over Germany, guided to their targets by *Oboe*-equipped PFF Mosquitoes and bombed with a precision seldom achieved by the main force heavies. Between January and May 1945, the LNSF Mosquitoes dropped 1,459 Blockbusters on Berlin alone and 1,500 on other targets.

Long Burning TI (LBTI) and Very Long Burning TI (VLBTI)

During the early *Oboe* raids, the shortest gap between Mosquito attacks was five minutes but to bridge any gaps in the marking a LBTI was developed. To fill the crucial 2-minute window when the candles had burned out, a staged device was produced. This was achieved with 20 candles igniting on the initial burst, another 20 after a 2½-minute delay and the final 20 after a 5-minute delay. In practice, a standard TI's life could be expanded up to seven minutes but, with fewer candles burning at the same time, their glow was less intense and often difficult to see. Further shuffling and extending of the ignition times could drag a TI's life to twelve minutes and these were called Very Long Burning TIs.

Long Stop   A ground marker, usually coloured yellow which was dropped to mark the edge of the area to bombed or stop the bombing from straying any further. Once dropped, this indicator would cancel out all stray TIs.

MB   Master Bomber

'Mossie'   Mosquito.

Musical   When *Oboe*-equipped Mosquitoes carried out the marking *Musical* was added as a prefix, for example *Musical Parramatta*.

Naxos   Enemy radar fitted to fighters which helped to home in on aircraft using H2S, *Fishpond* or *Monica*.

Newhaven   When flares were dropped high above the target area to illuminate it sufficiently so that PFF visual makers could operate.

Oboe   (See Appendix V)

Overture   Code name given to *Oboe* HE sorties

PAMPA   Photographic Reconnaissance and Meteorological Photography Aircraft, flown by 1407 Flight Mosquitoes from Oakington.

Parramatta   Involved the use of H2S radar or *Oboe* radio signals to aid the dropping of markers.

Pink Pansy   The Pink Pansy utilised a 4,000 lb bomb casing and was filled with the same ingredients as a Red Blob. This largest of all markers used by the PFF, actually weighed in at 2,800 lb and was used throughout the remainder of the war. A slight change in the colour made the device burn bright pink on impact.

PVM   Primary Visual Marker

Red Blob   First used on a raid against Nuremberg on 28/29 August 1942, the Red Blob was basically a 250 lb IB. An early rudimentary target marker, the incendiary was filled with a mixture of benzol, rubber and phosphorous, giving it a red glow when it burned.

Red Multi-flash TI

Used for the first time over Berlin on 23/24 November 1944 as route-markers but they did not stand out as clearly as normal TIs.

Red Spot Fire TI

These were first introduced over Peenemünde on the night of 17/18 August 1943. Bombing decoys placed by the enemy in order to detract from the main target were becoming increasingly successful by 1943 and this new TI attempted to rectify this problem. The TI used a 250 lb casing, filled with cotton wool soaked in metallic perchlorate, dissolved in alcohol. The TI was designed to burn as a single spot of red for up to 20 minutes although a green version was also introduced at a later stage. The spot fire that the TI created was easily obscured by smoke from bombing and so was only really used in any great quantity for smaller precision targets like Peenemünde. They were also ideally suited as route-markers but the problem of decoy fires was never completely solved.

Spoof   A separate attack, which grew in size as the war progressed, designed to draw enemy forces away from the main attack.

The 'Berlin Method'

From late 1943 onwards, PFF crews tended to carry *Wanganui* flares in case the target was cloud-covered; the policy changed for Berlin. PFF dropped both types of markers, irrespective of conditions over the target, and this became known as the 'Berlin Method'. The Main Force was briefed to bomb TIs when visible and only attack the *Wanganui* flares as a last resort. The Berlin method or technique was made official at a meeting on 20 December 1943.

TI   The first official TI used the standard and prolific 250 lb bomb casings. These were filled with 60 twelve-inch pyrotechnic candles fitting snugly inside the casing with a barometric fuse to eject them at 3,000 ft. Once free of the case, the candles cascaded to the ground where they burnt for three minutes.

From 3,000 ft the candles burned in an area approximately 100 yards across but this could be reduced to 60 yards when the ejection height was lowered to 1,500 ft. Colours used were red, green and yellow and the device's gross weight was 220 lbs. It was first used on a raid to Berlin on 16/17 January 1943.

Wanganui   Blind Skymarking by using *Oboe* or H2S to release TIs when target was obscured by cloud, haze or smoke.

Wimpie   A Wellington.

'Y' Aircraft   H2S equipped.

Appendix

VII

Abbreviations

AASF Advanced Air Striking Force

ACM Air Chief Marshal

ADLS Air Delivery Letter Services

AI Airborne Interception

Air Cdre
    Air Commodore

AM Air Marshal

AOC Air Officer Commanding

ASI Air Speed Indicator

AVM Air Vice Marshal

Brig Brigadier

Capt Captain

CO Commanding Officer

CU Conversion Unit

DB Disbanded

DFC Distinguished Flying Cross

DFM Distinguished Flying Medal

DSO Distinguished Service Order

ETA Estimated Time of Arrival

Fg Off
    Flying Officer

Flt Lt Flight Lieutenant

Flt Sgt
    Flight Sergeant

FTS Flying Training School

GCI Ground Control Interception

Gen General

Gp Capt
    Group Captain

HC High Capacity

HCU Heavy Conversion Unit

HE High Explosive

HQ Headquarters

IB Incendiary Bomb

Kg Kampfgruppe

LBTI Long Burning Target Indicator

Lt Lieutenant

Mjr Major

MPI Mean Point of Impact

MTU Mosquito Training Unit

NJG Nachtjagdeschwader

NTU Navigation Training Unit

Oblt Oberleutnant

QFI Qualified Flying Instructor

ORB Operational Records Book

OTU Operational Training Unit

PFF Pathfinder Force

Plt Off

Pilot Officer

PRU Photographic Reconnaissance

RAAF Royal Australian Air Force

RCAF Royal Canadian Air Force

RFC Royal Flying Corps

RF Reformed

RDF Radar Direction Finding

Sgt Sergeant

SOC Struck Off Charge

Sqn Squadron

Sqn Ldr

Squadron Leader

TAF Tactical Air Force

US United States

VC Victoria Cross

Wg Cdr

Wing Commander

WIDU Wireless Intelligence Development Unit

Index

The RAF Pathfinders

Bomber Command's Elite Squadrons

The formation of the Pathfinder Force in August 1942 produced a steady but certain change in the fortunes of Bomber Command. During the early years of the war, aerial photographs showed that less than one third of the aircraft were successfully placing their bombs with accuracy. There was a basic lack of navigation skills, as well as what came to be known in the RAF as the will to 'Press On'.

These shortcomings were addressed, and the special force of elite aircrew, the Pathfinder squadrons, whose purpose was to locate targets and mark them, proved indispensible to the success of the RAF's overall bombing campaign.

Led by the inspirational and imaginative Don Bennett, Pathfinders were equipped with the best available aircraft, which included the famous Lancaster bomber and later, increasingly, the Mosquito. To join a Pathfinder squadron (all crewmen were volunteers) was a rare privilege but with it went a huge leap in the likelihood of being shot down. Pathfinder aircraft led the way for their following bomber force in hazardous raid after raid. They were highly vulnerable to the wall of flak thrown up by German city defenders, as well as to attacks by night-fighters; and it took a full 25 minutes to run the gauntlet of the Berlin defences from end to end at full stretch. By the end of the war, some 56,000 crewmen of Bomber Command had lost their lives.

Martyn Chorlton has written a gripping account of the RAF's Pathfinder squadrons, recalling the often reckless heroism of the young aircrew and the challenges they faced in the smoke-filled skies over occupied Europe. His book also contains a moving foreword by Michael Wadsworth, chaplain to the Pathfinders Association.

ISBN 978 1 84674 201 9

9 781846 742019

£14.95
www.countrysidebooks.co.uk

IMAGES
of America
JOHNSON COUNTY

Mollie Gallop Bradbury Mims